Daily Writing Reinforcers™

Teacher's Resource Manual
Grade 3

Authors

Carolyn R. Sullivan

Philip L. Skoglund

Chet H. Melcher

Jeffrey J. Blaga

Vernon Hills, Illinois

Thank you for purchasing the Daily Reinforcers™ Program.

At ETA, we are dedicated to insuring your satisfaction with our products. Please call us at 800-445-5985, or write to us at the address below to share your suggestions, comments, questions, or concerns about the Daily Reinforcers Program with us. We look forward to hearing from you!

The ETA Staff

Cover Design: Chad Rich and Thomas Greene
Art: Some images herein are used with the permission of Zedcor, Inc., Tucson, AZ.

Daily Writing Reinforcers—Grade 3
ISBN 0-7406-0065-6

ETA, 620 Lakeview Parkway
Vernon Hills, Illinois 60061-1838

©1999, GRØW Publications. All rights reserved. No part of this publication may be reproduced or transmitted in any form or by any means, electronic or mechanical, including photocopying, recording, or any information storage and retrieval system, without permission in writing from GRØW Publications and ETA, the publisher. Permission is hereby granted to reproduce the blackline masters, indicated by a copyright notice on each activity, for classroom use only and not for resale.

Printed in the United States of America

Overview of Daily Writing

Thank you for choosing *Daily Writing*.

Daily Writing was developed by a team of practicing classroom teachers and administrators using an approach similar to the one that led to the creation of *Daily Reading*, *Arithmetic Developed Daily (ADD)*, *Daily Geography* and *Daily Science*, programs that are now in use in schools throughout the United States.

This program was developed to assist students with learning to use the writing process as a communication tool, and with incorporating writing skills into their daily written work. The ultimate goal of this program is to produce writers who are aware that writing is an important way to organize their thinking and to communicate with a larger audience. *Daily Writing* sets forth a consistent and comprehensive approach to learning, and all in a format students enjoy. On a daily basis, your students will encounter information, strategies and skills that will insure their retention and understanding of the conventions and thought processes that are used when producing written language.

Daily Writing is a program based on current research in writing as well as what good teachers know about the importance of daily reinforcement and continual application of skills being learned. The writing process, including prewriting, drafting, revising, editing/proofreading, and publishing is an important thinking process and real-life skill. Many types of writing are addressed in the program including personal narrative, letter writing, fiction, nonfiction, biography, poetry, essay, autobiography and news reporting.

Program Design

Daily Writing can be used as a warm-up activity as you begin your writing lesson, regardless of the writing approach you use in your classroom. The Grade 1 manual includes 129 activities, while manuals for Grades 2 through 6 contain 144 activities. In the teacher section you will find answers to the exercises, as well as explicit instructions on how to introduce the strategy, process, or skill(s) being emphasized. Your manual also includes background information and ideas on how you can extend and reinforce many of these warm-up activities.

Using Daily Writing

Daily Writing allows you to get your writing lesson off to a challenging start. It is recommended that the program be used with every writing lesson. The short activities, used on a regular basis, generate the maximum retention of knowledge and skills.

Daily Writing was designed with a variety of teaching styles and needs in mind. The activities in Grades 1 and 2 should be used in the order in which they appear in the manuals. The program is highly developmental and often one activity adds to or reinforces a previous one. However, the exercises in Grades 3-6 can be used to coordinate with a focus you have targeted for a given day or set of days in your regular writing program. The detailed scope and sequence allows you to select activities to reinforce specific skills, such as ending punctuation, to support your area of focus.

Implementation of the program is easy, with at least four ways in which you can use the activities.

1. Duplicate an activity strip for each student in your classroom using the blackline masters in the book. Students complete the work on the strip, occasionally extending work to the back of the sheet.
2. Use the *Daily Writing* diary approach. Write the daily exercises on the board or a blank transparency (or use the pre-printed transparency available from GRØW Publications), and encourage students to keep a diary by writing each answer in their notebooks.

3. Project the exercises on transparencies available from GRØW Publications along with distributing a duplicated activity strip to each student. Students can do the work on their duplicated strips and then you or your students work through the activity on the overhead for the entire class.
4. Allow students to complete each exercise in their personal "Check-Up" booklets, available from GRØW Publications. Each strip is already duplicated and assembled into a checkbook style workbook for each student.

You may choose to complete the daily exercises with the entire class or have students work individually or cooperatively with each task. A student can be called on to share an answer and provide information on how he/she accomplished the task. Teachers are encouraged to expand upon students' responses and provide additional insight into the content/skill areas being developed. As previously noted, ample background information and instructional suggestions are provided to the teacher on the "Teacher Notes" page for most of the daily activities.

Starting with Grade 2, necessary answers appear first on the teacher's pages, usually in bold face type. In some instances, there will be no one right answer and the phrase, "Answers will vary" appears in the appropriate place on the teacher page. With these activities, you will often be given a number of suggested responses which can be used to assist students. Key words to be emphasized with students have been underlined in the teacher comment section for easy reference.

Writing Process and Skill Areas

Daily Writing covers the following six general areas.

1. **The Writing Process**
   Prewriting - thinking processes students utilize to organize information before drafting.
   Drafting - the actual writing of a story, article, letter, etc.
   Revising - looking again at your writing. This may include reorganizing, deleting, adding or changing information to make the piece of writing clearer and/or more interesting to an audience. Revision can occur at any time in the writing process.
   Proofreading/Editing - using the punctuation, capitalization, and grammatical conventions of the written language.
   Publishing - preparing a piece of writing for a larger audience.

2. **Author's Craft** - studying and using the various qualities of good writing which make a reader want to read further. These include using descriptive language, leads, endings, dialogue, etc.

3. **Mechanics** - the conventions of the written language including capitalization, punctuation and paragraph format.

4. **Parts of Speech** - the manner in which words in the English language are categorized.

5. **Grammar/Usage** - using words properly when writing.

6. **Sentences** - types of sentences, parts of a sentence, and the structure of sentences in the English language.

A specified number of exercises representing these areas have been sequentially placed throughout *Daily Writing*. The areas used with each daily exercise are clearly identified on the teacher page.

This program will engage your students in a wide range of communication processes that integrate speaking, reading and writing. *Daily Writing* will reinforce and enhance whatever regular classroom writing program you are using.

Daily Writing Authors

Carolyn R. Sullivan holds a Master of Arts in Education with an emphasis in reading curriculum and instruction from the University of Colorado-Boulder. She has been a classroom teacher, reading specialist, staff developer, and is currently a Title I Language Arts Specialist in the Adams Twelve Five Star Schools in Northglenn, Colorado.

Philip L. Skoglund earned a Master of Science degree from the University of Wisconsin-Milwaukee and is currently a classroom teacher and subject area coordinator for the Racine (Wisconsin) Unified School District. He has taught at various educational levels.

Jeffrey J. Blaga earned a doctorate in education from The Ohio State University and has taught middle, high school and college classes in Ohio, Iowa and Wisconsin. He is the co-author of numerous educational materials.

Chet H. Melcher is a Supervisor of Curriculum and Instruction for the Racine (Wisconsin) Unified School District. He holds a Master of Education degree from the University of Wisconsin - Whitewater and has taught middle, high school and college level courses for over two decades.

Daily Writing Scope and Sequence

The tables on the following pages show where writing skills are introduced and reinforced at each Grade level. Each exercise in *Daily Writing* includes the general rubric under which the problem falls. This information is always included on the corresponding teacher pages for quick review by the teacher.

Daily Writing Genres in Grade 3

This chart identifies the genres addressed throughout the *Daily Writing* activities at Grade 3 and lists specific activities in which they can be found. These charts are provided for Grades 3-6 in the *Daily Writing* program.

Genre	*Activities*
Personal Narrative	15, 30, 57, 83, 84, 85, 114, 124, 125, 141
Character Development	14, 40, 63, 116
Letters	81
Description	12, 13, 113, 114
Fiction	19, 62, 115
Nonfiction	46, 76, 77, 78, 79, 89, 100
Math	139
News Report	97, 98, 99
Autobiography	119
Note-taking	77, 78
Self Assessment	144

Daily Writing Scope and Sequence

I = introduced   R = reinforced

WRITING PROCESS

	Grade 3 Activities	1	2	3	4	5	6
Prewriting							
Drawing		I	R				
Brainstorming	4, 48, 76, 97, 124	I	R	R	R	R	R
Mapping/Clustering	14, 40, 84, 98	I	R	R	R	R	R
Topic Selection	3, 47, 57, 83, 109, 119	I	R	R	R	R	R
Form Selection	81, 97, 108, 140		I	R	R	R	R
Note-taking	77, 78			I	R	R	R
Outlining					I	R	R
Drafting							
Writing Development - Capital and Small Letters		I	R				
Writing Development - Spaces/Words		I	R				
Writing Development - Consonants	21	I	R	R			
Writing Development - Vowels	22	I	R	R	R		
Consonant Blends		I	R	R	R		
Consonant Digraphs		I	R	R			
Word Endings		I	R	R	R	R	R
Organized Structure	15, 57, 119	I	R	R	R	R	R
Topics Developed with Details	12, 13, 37, 79, 124	I	R	R	R	R	R
Focused Message	6, 45	I	R	R	R	R	R
Revising							
Story Makes Sense	6, 36, 120, 136, 137	I	R	R	R	R	R
Revision Strategies	36-7, 55-6, 68, 111, 136-7	I	R	R	R	R	R
Proofreading/Editing							
Standard Grammar	23, 58, 134	I	R	R	R	R	R
Spelling	10, 44, 82	I	R	R	R	R	R
Punctuation	7, 31, 51, 92	I	R	R	R	R	R
Capitalization	7, 31, 50, 92, 105	I	R	R	R	R	R
Standard Editing Notation	90, 130			I	R	R	R

AUTHOR'S CRAFT

	Grade 3 Activities	1	2	3	4	5	6
Descriptive Language							
Descriptive Language	28, 30, 113, 114			I	R	R	R

Daily Writing Scope and Sequence

I = introduced   R = reinforced

Strong Verbs

Strong Verbs	29, 30, 74, 127		I	R	R	R	R

Creative Leads

Creative Leads	5, 46, 85, 125		I	R	R	R	R

Creative Endings

Creative Endings	38, 86, 126, 135			I	R	R	R

Titles

Titles	39, 91, 128, 135		I	R	R	R	R

Organizational Pattern

Beginning, Middle, End	15, 57, 141		I	R	R	R	R	R
Problem, Events, Solution	19, 62, 115				I	R	R	R
Topic Sentence, Details	99, 100, 101, 102				I	R	R	R

Dialogue

Dialogue	25, 26, 52, 121, 131			I	R	R	R

Figurative Language

Figurative Language	59, 117			I	R	R	R

Develops Story Characters

Develops Story Characters	40, 63, 116			I	R	R	R

MECHANICS

	Grade 3 Activities	1	2	3	4	5	6

Capitalization

Pronoun I	41, 64, 66	I	R	R	R		
Beginning of Sentence	41, 64, 133	I	R	R	R		
Proper Noun	9, 41, 65, 66, 106	I	R	R	R	R	
Direct Quote	50, 51, 64, 121, 131			I	R	R	R
Greeting and Closing of a Letter	75, 80, 81, 132		I	R	R	R	

Punctuation

End of Sentence (. ! ?)	8, 60, 122, 133	I	R	R	R	R	R
Comma	20, 75, 80		I	R	R	R	
Apostrophe	24, 70		I	R	R	R	
Quotation Mark	25, 26, 49, 52	I	R	R	R	R	
Colon						I	R
Italics and Underlining						I	R

Daily Writing Scope and Sequence

I = introduced   R = reinforced

Paragraphing

			1	2	3	4	5	6
Indenting	71, 72, 73, 130				I	R	R	R
Paragraph Structure	71, 72, 89, 90				I	R	R	R
Dialogue	90				I	R	R	R

PARTS OF SPEECH

	Grade 3 Activities		1	2	3	4	5	6

Noun

			1	2	3	4	5	6
Common Noun	18, 35		I	R	R	R	R	R
Proper Noun	18, 67, 129			I	R	R	R	R
Singular and Plural Nouns	35		I	R	R	R	R	R
Possessive Noun	24, 70, 96, 103				I	R	R	R

Pronoun

			1	2	3	4	5	6
Pronoun	53, 95			I	I	R	R	R

Adjective

			1	2	3	4	5	6
Adjective	61, 138				I	R	R	R

Adverb

			1	2	3	4	5	6
Adverb						I	R	R

Preposition

			1	2	3	4	5	6
Preposition							I	R

Verb

			1	2	3	4	5	6
Verb	29, 88			I	R	R	R	R

GRAMMAR/USAGE

	Grade 3 Activities		1	2	3	4	5	6

Verb Tense

			1	2	3	4	5	6
Verb Tense	88		I	R	R	R	R	R

Subject/Verb Agreement

			1	2	3	4	5	6
Subject/Verb Agreement	23, 27		I	R	R	R	R	R

Homophones/Homographs

			1	2	3	4	5	6
Homophones/Homographs	33, 34, 139			I	R	R	R	R

Antonyms

			1	2	3	4	5	6
Antonyms	32, 93		I	R	R	R	R	R

Synonyms

			1	2	3	4	5	6
Synonyms	54, 94			I	R	R	R	R

Daily Writing Scope and Sequence

I = introduced   R = reinforced

Contractions

Contractions	16, 92		I	R	R	R	R

Compound Words

Compound Words	69		I	R	R	R	R

Double Negatives

Double Negatives	27, 95				I	R	R	R

Naming Self Last

Naming Self Last	17, 95		I	R	R	R	R

SENTENCES

	Grade 3 Activities	1	2	3	4	5	6
Types							
Declarative	42, 43, 123	I	R	R	R	R	R
Interrogative	42, 43, 123	I	R	R	R	R	R
Exclamatory	42, 43, 123	I	R	R	R	R	R
Imperative	123			I	R	R	R
Parts							
Subject	87, 118			I	R	R	R
Predicate	87, 118			I	R	R	R
Direct Object					I	R	R
Structure							
Complete Sentences	11, 104	I	R	R	R	R	R
Sentence Fragments	11, 104	I	R	R	R	R	R
Run-on Sentences	31, 112	I	R	R	R	R	R
Simple Sentences	118	I	R	R	R	R	R
Compound Sentences					I	R	R

ASSESSMENT

	Grade 3 Activities	1	2	3	4	5	6
Student/Teacher Assessment							
Student and Teacher Assessment	1, 2, 47, 107, 108, 110, 111,	I	R	R	R	R	R
Student and Teacher Assessment (cont.)	142, 143, 144	I	R	R	R	R	R

Daily Writing 3

Name _____

There are many different types of writing. Some are listed in the chart below. On the top, tell how often you do that type of writing. On the bottom, tell how much you enjoy that type of writing. Circle **L** for lots, **S** for sometimes and **N** for never.

How often you write it →	L S N	L S N	L S N	L S N	L S N
TYPE of WRITING	Personal Narrative	Fiction	Poetry	Nonfiction	Letters
How much you enjoy it →	L S N	L S N	L S N	L S N	L S N

© GRØW Publications

Daily Writing 3

Name _____   © GRØW Publications

Match these writing skills with the box that best describes your writing.

- Capitalizing words
- Using ending marks (. ! ?)
- Spelling

- I'm good at it!
- I do okay.
- I'm working on it.

- Using complete sentences
- Commas in dates, letters
- Talk marks (" ")
- Rereading my stories

Daily Writing 3

Name _____   © GRØW Publications

In the next two minutes, list all the things you could write about. The words in the box might help.

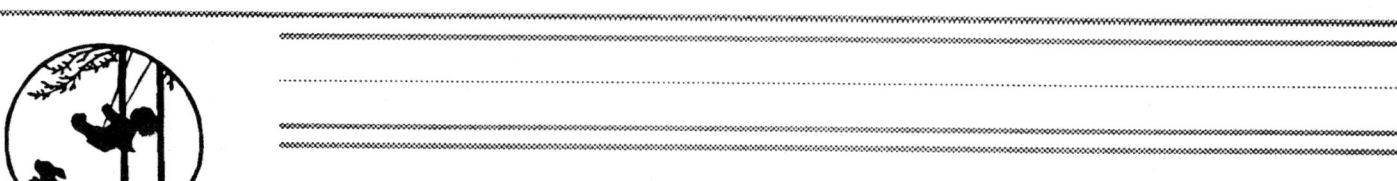

| PEOPLE | PLACES | HOBBIES | INTERESTS | TRIPS | POEMS | LETTERS |
| OPINIONS | EVENTS | IMAGINARY STORIES | IDEAS | THINGS TO INVESTIGATE |

Teacher Notes - DAILY WRITING - Grade 3

Answers/Comments | 1

Students can use the backs of their activity strips to complete the daily problems or to work on extension exercises. For this lesson, ask your students to make a list of the various things they wrote about in second grade on the reverse sides of their activity strips. This exercise will help you assess the kinds of writing your students have done and what they prefer to write. This information is important because it will help you encourage them to try something different in their writing. For example, the person with a strong poetic voice should also be writing non-fiction reports.

Topics Student/Teacher Assessment
Student and Teacher Assessment

Answers/Comments | 2

Student responses will vary.
This is an assessment activity that targets writing skills. If you have a beginning of the year assessment that includes a graded writing sample, it will be interesting to compare a student's perception of his/her writing skills to the skills used in the writing sample. Remind your students that the purpose of using correct grammar, capitalization, punctuation, and spelling is so the reader will not be distracted from the author's message by incorrect writing skills.

Topics Student/Teacher Assessment
Student and Teacher Assessment

Answers/Comments | 3

Instruct your students to use the backs of their activity strips to continue their lists if they run out of room. Make sure they understand they are not to copy the words in the box. They are to think of specific things about which they can write. If time permits, discuss the words in the box with your students. Ideas/opinions may range all the way from things that "bug" you, to ideas about love, kindness, sadness, friends, etc. If students need help with the term "events," inform them that events are experiences a person has had. An event can be observations from a moment in time or stretched over several hours or days.

Topics Writing Process
Prewriting
Topic Selection

Permission granted to copy student pages for purchaser's class. It is unlawful to copy the teacher materials.
© GRØW Publications

DAILY WRITING 3

Name _____ © GROW Publications

4

Choose one of the topics you listed in Activity 3. Make a list of what you would include if you wrote a story about that topic.

TOPIC: _____

1 _____
2 _____
3 _____
4 _____
5 _____
6 _____
7 _____

DAILY WRITING 3

Name _____ © GROW Publications

5

Use your list from Activity 4 to think of 2 good beginnings or leads for your story.

1 _____

2 _____

DAILY WRITING 3

Name _____

6

This story doesn't make sense. Can you fix it?

Sister Trouble

I have brand new baby sister. Most of the time he's pretty good but sometimes I can't believe the things she does. When we eat oatmeal for she tips the bowl upside down on her head. My friend, Joe, has 2 sisters. My sister grabs my hair and won't let go. She thinks it's funny silly. She laughs and laughs.

© GROW Publications

Teacher Notes - DAILY WRITING - Grade 3

Answers/Comments [4]

Individual student responses will vary. Making a list of ideas such as students are doing in this exercise, is one way to use brainstorming. Brainstorming helps students retrieve information they have mentally stored about a topic or incident. Your students will be using this list in Activity 5. You may want to establish the expectation in your classroom that your students will "plan" each of the stories they write. Their plans may be in the form of a list, mapping, clustering, KW of KWL (What I know, What I want to know, What I learned), a story map, etc.

Topics
Writing Process
Prewriting
Brainstorming

Answers/Comments [5]

Student leads will vary. Ask students what they know about what a lead is. What does a good lead do for a piece of writing? Reinforce the information the class might have learned from past writing activities. A good lead hooks the reader, it makes them want to read on. A good lead is a promise of what is to come. Extend this exercise by asking your students to look in many different books and identify good leads, bad leads and those in between. Try completing such an exercise in pairs, sharing the best and worst leads the class finds.

Topics
Author's Craft
Creative Leads

Answers/Comments [6]

Answers may include:
1. have <u>a</u> brand new
2. time <u>she's</u> pretty good
3. oatmeal for <u>breakfast</u>
4. take out the part about Joe's sisters
5. <u>funny</u> or <u>silly</u>, not both

This activity will give you an idea of your students' ability to proofread a story. You may want them to work in pairs or in small groups. Revision means to see (vision) a piece or writing again (re). Since almost all writing is intended to be read, the writer must be considerate of the reader.

Topics
Writing Process
Drafting
Focused Message

Writing Process
Revising
Story Makes Sense

Permission granted to copy student pages for purchaser's class. <u>It is unlawful</u> to copy the teacher materials.
© GRØW Publications

Daily Writing 3

Name _____ © GROW Publications   7

The capitals and ending marks are missing in the sentences below. Add . ! and ? as needed. Circle the letters that should be capitalized and write the correct letter above them.

Hairy Decisions

i have been thinking about getting my hair cut for days   first i think i should get it cut short   next i think i think i should let the top grow   he's ready to go   i have to decide   oh no

---

Daily Writing 3

Name _____ © GROW Publications   8

Explain why you would use each of these ending marks.

.
!
?

Daily Writing 3

Name _____ © GROW Publications   9

Decide whether each of the following needs a capital letter at the beginning of the word. If so, give an example.

1. Y N Months of the year
2. Y N Tools
3. Y N People's names
4. Y N Days of the week
5. Y N Zoo animals
6. Y N Holidays
7. Y N Seasons of the year

Teacher Notes - DAILY WRITING - Grade 3

Answers/Comments — 7

I; days. First; short. Next I; ~~I think~~; I should; grow. H; go. I; decide. Oh no!

If there is time remaining, ask your students to write on the back of their activity strips a short story about their hair. Stress the importance of being able to put in capitals and ending marks as students are writing their drafts. Review, with your students, the criteria for a sentence.
  1. A sentence begins with a capital, and ends with a (.) (!) or (?).
  2. A sentence is a group of words that expresses a complete thought.

Topics
Writing Process
Proofreading/Editing
Punctuation, Capitalization

Answers/Comments — 8

Student explanations will vary. Discuss the three ending marks, stressing their importance in both reading and writing. After students explain when each mark should be used, instruct them to write three sentences using a different ending mark for each one. They can do this on the backs of their activity strips or on separate pieces of paper.

Topics
Mechanics
Punctuation
End of Sentence (. ! ?)

Answers/Comments — 9

1. Yes 2. No 3. Yes 4. Yes 5. No 6. Yes 7. No

Through their writing activities in Grades 1 and 2, your students should remember that months, days, holidays, people's names, and the word I are always capitalized. Investigate what other items your students can add to the list. Space permitting, keep an ongoing chart of the words that need to be capitalized for the class to refer to as they are writing.

Topics
Mechanics
Capitalization
Proper Noun

Permission granted to copy student pages for purchaser's class. It is unlawful to copy the teacher materials.
© GROW Publications

DAILY WRITING 3

Name _____ © GROW Publications

10

Circle the words that are spelled incorrectly. Write the correct spelling above the misspelled word. Use the words in the box to help you.

again	care	coach	could	each	every	have
hear	mine	my	of	over	play	went	when

Baseball is mi life. I pla baseball evry summer. Ech year I hav a new coch. I don't understand why mi old coch always quits at the end ov the season wen he culd be coaching me again.

DAILY WRITING 3

Name _____ © GROW Publications

11

What is a sentence? _____

_____

Change the sentences below so they are complete sentences.

My dog is just. _____

We took our dog swimming at the lake. _____

Then saved a little girl. _____

DAILY WRITING 3

Name _____ © GROW Publications

12

Choose a place you know a lot about. Circle one of the choices or make up your own.

grocery store   school   movie theater   museum   park   zoo   _____
my choice

Close your eyes and picture the place you chose. Write down everything you see.

_____
_____
_____
_____
_____

Teacher Notes - DAILY WRITING - Grade 3

Answers/Comments   **10**

Answers:	my	play	every
	Each	have	coach
	my	coach	of
	when	could	

Circling incorrectly spelled words and writing the correct spelling above the identified word is the same method used in previous grades. Encourage your students to use this method for targeting misspelled words in their written work. Students should also have dictionaries available when proofreading/editing.

Topics
Writing Process
Proofreading/Editing
Spelling

Answers/Comments   **11**

A sentence is a group of words that expresses an idea. It begins with a capital letter and ends with a (.) (?) or (!). Students should make complete sentences for the three examples on their sheets.

Take the time to explain the terms <u>complete sentence</u> and <u>sentence fragment</u> to your students. Ask for volunteers to make up a sentence or sentence fragment and share it with the class. The class can then decide which one it is.

Topics
Sentences
Structure
Complete Sentences, Sentence Fragments

Answers/Comments   **12**

Student responses will vary. Third grade is a wonderful year to watch young writers grow. They move from writing about simple action and bed to bed stories to using description and writing in varied forms (fiction, letters, poetry, nonfiction, etc.). Encourage your young writers to think more like authors. This activity helps them to transport their readers to a place with which they, the authors, are familiar. They will be using what they have written here in the following exercise.

Topics
Writing Process
Drafting
Topics Developed with Details

Permission granted to copy student pages for purchaser's class. <u>It is unlawful</u> to copy the teacher materials.
© GRØW Publications

DAILY WRITING 3

Name _____ © GRØW Publications 13

Using your list from Activity 12, write a description of the place you chose.

_____
_____
_____
_____
_____
_____
_____

DAILY WRITING 3

Name _____ © GRØW Publications 14

Think of a person about whom you would have fun writing. Write the following information.

Who is it? _____

How he or she looks
_____
_____

How he or she acts
_____
_____

What he or she says
_____

DAILY WRITING 3

Name _____ 15

In Activity 14, you chose a person and started thinking about what he or she is like. Today, think about a time you were together. Draw what happened at the beginning, middle, and end of that time.

BEGINNING	MIDDLE	END

© GRØW Publications

Teacher Notes - DAILY WRITING - Grade 3

Answers/Comments — 13

Student descriptions will vary. If there is not enough room for your students to finish their paragraphs, direct them to use the backs of the activity strips or separate pieces of paper. It is important to see is whether or not their descriptions build a picture in the reader's mind. Conclude this activity by dividing your students into pairs, and have each student read the descriptive paragraph to his/her partner. Instruct the partners to either listen carefully and tell your partner what you see, or draw a picture that goes with the author's words.

Topics
Writing Process
Drafting
Topics Developed with Details

Answers/Comments — 14

The information students choose to include will vary. Your students will need the information they wrote in this exercise for Activity 15. Instead of just thinking randomly, this activity is organized to help students plan some of the things they may want to include in a story about a person they know. Categorizing items in this manner is a form of mapping. In preparation for tomorrow's warm-up, request that your students begin thinking about a time they remember being with this person.

Topics
Writing Process
Prewriting
Mapping/Clustering

Answers/Comments — 15

Student responses will vary. Encourage your students to use the information they wrote in Activity 14 and integrate it into the story they have planned today. Many of your students will be writing using a beginning and details for the middle. Endings seem to be a more difficult concept for third graders. Students will have extended opportunities to practice this concept later in this grade level. Many of your students may choose to write about their special person during their regular writing time today.

Topics
Writing Process   **Author's Craft**
Drafting   Organizational Pattern
Organized structure   Beginning, Middle, End

Permission granted to copy student pages for purchaser's class. It is unlawful to copy the teacher materials.
© GRØW Publications

DAILY WRITING 3

Name _____ 16

Underline the two words in each sentence that can be written as a contraction. Write the contraction above the two words.

Ring, Ring, Ring

My brother is not little. He is 16. It is fun when he gets phone calls. I will run to the phone and answer it. It is almost always a girl. I politely say, " He will be here in just a minute." Then I scream down the stairs, "Evan, it is for you." Then I put down the phone and I am off like a bolt of lightning.

© GROW Publications

DAILY WRITING 3

Name _____ © GROW Publications 17

Write three sentences that tell three different things you have done with three different people. Be sure to include the person's name in each one.

1. _____

2. _____

3. _____

DAILY WRITING 3

Name _____ 18

Nouns are words that name a person, place or thing. **Proper nouns** name a special person, place or thing. Complete the table below.

Common Noun	day		dog	
Proper Noun			St. Bernard	

Common Noun		holiday		school
Proper Noun	September		Iowa	

© GROW Publications

Teacher Notes - DAILY WRITING - Grade 3

Answers/Comments | 16 |

1. isn't 2. he's 3. it's 4. I'll 5. it's 6. he'll 7. it's 8. I'm

It is important for students to learn how contractions are formed. Since students are usually encouraged to write in a natural voice, contractions are often a part of everyday thinking and talking. If your students finish quickly, ask them to write as many contractions as they can on the backs of their activity strips.

Topics Grammar/Usage
Contractions

Answers/Comments | 17 |

Students sentences will vary. Either remind your students that the other person's name should come first, or let them proceed without any additional information. Compare these sentences with your class:

Me and mom went shopping.   *Mom and I went shopping.*

Which one sounds better? Mention to them that it is polite to always use the other person's name first. Moreover, share your expectation that they will use this knowledge in the writing they do every day.

Topics Grammar/Usage
Naming Self Last

Answers/Comments | 18 |

Student responses will vary, and please note that any proper nouns should be capitalized. If students finish quickly, ask them to write two proper nouns to match the common noun. It is important for students to realize that proper nouns are capitalized. For this reason, knowing what a noun and proper noun are is information that will not only help your students classify words in the English language, but will also help them know which words need capital letters.

Topics Parts of Speech
Noun
Common Noun, Proper Noun

Permission granted to copy student pages for purchaser's class. It is unlawful to copy the teacher materials.
© GRØW Publications

Teacher Notes - DAILY WRITING - Grade 3

Answers/Comments — 19

Student responses will vary. In this activity, encourage your students to spend time visualizing the old house and then write using descriptive words to build a similar picture in the reader's mind. Fiction stories are often organized using the structure found in this exercise. This is one of the ways that reading supports writing and writing supports reading. It aids in reading comprehension to know there is an organizational pattern to a story.

Topics
Author's Craft
Organizational Pattern
Problem, Events, Solution

Answers/Comments — 20

Answer: To tell the reader to pause.
1. Dear Jackie,   2. Your friend, Larry   3. October 1, 1996
4. I like peas, beans, squash, broccoli and onions.
5. Columbus, Ohio

Commas give a reader the signal to pause momentarily while reading. They help the reader make sense of the author's message. Be sure your students understand that not only should they be able to place commas correctly in the places in the activity, they should be able to do it in their own writing.

Topics
Mechanics
Punctuation
Comma

Answers/Comments — 21

Student choices of words will vary. Review the terms consonants and vowels with your students. They should be able to use the digraphs ch, sh, th, and wh fluently in their writing. See if the class remembers that blends are two or more letters, that when put together, make a new sound of their own. For example, you don't say "s," "q," "u," you blend them together to say "squ."

Topics
Writing Process
Drafting
Writing Development - Consonants

DAILY WRITING 3

Name _____ © GROW Publications   22

Read these words: **slim - slime, Tim - time, mad - made, fat - fate**

As you look at each pair of words, what changes?

As you read each pair of words, what changes?

How can knowing this help you when you write?

DAILY WRITING 3

Name _____   23

This story sounds funny. Rewrite it, changing what you need to so that it sounds like correct grammar.

I seen the biggest lollipop yesterday. It sitted in the window of a candy store. I goed in to buy it. The lady said it costed $1.50. I got just enough money. Now I'll have to talk my mom into letting me ate it.

© GROW Publications

DAILY WRITING 3

Name _____ © GROW Publications   24

This is a comma. ——   This is an apostrophe. ——

Finish the 3 sentences.

pencil is
Use the name of a friend.

| **Apostrophes** are used to show ownership. Examples: the boy's lunch the dog's dish the baby's toy |

The _____ house is
Use the name of an animal.

desk is
Use the name of your teacher.

Teacher Notes - DAILY WRITING - Grade 3

Answers/Comments — 22

1. An "e" was added to each of the words.
2. In the first words, the vowel sounds are short. After adding the "e," the middle vowel sound became long.
3. A suggested student response: It helps me know how to spell words better.

Remember, the silent "e" vowel rule holds 85% of the time or more. It is a very useful rule to know.

Topics

Writing Process
Drafting
Writing Development - Vowels

Answers/Comments — 23

Student rewritten stories will vary. These words need to be changed: seen –> saw; sitted –> sat; goed –> went; costed –> cost; got –> had; ate –> eat. Explain the term <u>grammar</u> to your students. It is the study of words and how they are used in a sentence. Instruct your students to write their sentences on other pieces of paper or in their *Daily Writing* notebook, if appropriate. If you are short on time today, you may want your students to cross out incorrect words and then write the words that sound better above them.

Topics

Writing Process
Proofreading/Editing
Standard Grammar

Grammar/Usage
Subject/Verb Agreement

Answers/Comments — 24

Students' answers should reflect an understanding of the concepts. This activity only deals with singular possessives. Later, in *Daily Writing*, you will be focusing on both singular and plural possessives. Inquire with your class as to what other kinds of words need apostrophes. Apostrophes are used in contractions to show that a letter or letters is/are missing. Challenge your students to be looking throughout the day in their reading and writing to find words that show ownership.

Topics

Mechanics
Punctuation
Apostrophe

Parts of speech
Noun
Possessive Noun

Permission granted to copy student pages for purchaser's class. <u>It is unlawful</u> to copy the teacher materials.
© GRØW Publications

DAILY WRITING 3

25

Name _____

When a writer wants to show that someone is talking, what kind of punctuation marks does he or she use?

_____

Here is a conversation between two boys and a talking giraffe. Finish writing this conversation.

"Giraffes are my favorite animal," said Cisco.

"Mine, too!" said Tim.

"I have a great idea. Let's get out of here," said the giraffe.

© GRØW Publications

DAILY WRITING 3

26

Name _____ © GRØW Publications

Think of a person you had a conversation with lately. Answer these questions.

Who was it? _____

What was it about? _____

Where was it? _____

Write some of your conversation. Be sure to use "talk" (quotation) marks.

DAILY WRITING 3

27

Name _____

In each set, fill in the circle of the sentence that sounds like it is correct.

1. ○ My mom takes me in the car.
    ○ I takes the bus.
    ○ They has to walk.

2. ○ I don't get no prize.
    ○ We don't get no prizes.
    ○ They don't get any prizes.

3. ○ She won't want no candy.
    ○ He won't want any candy.
    ○ They won't want no candy.

4. ○ We is looking at the mouse.
    ○ They looks at the mouse.
    ○ He is looking at the mouse.

Teacher Notes - DAILY WRITING - Grade 3

Answers/Comments — 25

Students' work will vary. Request that each student continue the conversation on a separate piece of paper or on the back of his or her activity strip. You may have a few students who need to be reminded of what the term conversation means. Be sure they notice where the quotation marks, commas, and periods are placed. Encourage your students to use conversation in the stories they are writing. Authors use conversation because it helps characters come alive to the reader, or carries the action forward.

Topics
Mechanics
Punctuation
Quotation Mark

Author's Craft
Dialogue

Answers/Comments — 26

Student responses to these questions will vary according to the person selected. Each student will need to use the back of the activity strip or a separate sheet of paper to complete this exercise. As noted earlier, a notebook set aside to complete *Daily Writing* activities is helpful because they are all in the same place. If there is time, allow some of your students to share their conversations. Be sure students notice if any of the conversations reveal what the person may be like in real life.

Topics
Mechanics
Punctuation
Quotation Mark

Author's Craft
Dialogue

Answers/Comments — 27

1. My mom takes me in the car.
2. They don't get any prizes.
3. He won't want any candy.
4. He is looking at the mouse.

This activity highlights subject/verb agreement and double negatives. Writers avoid sentences having two negative words in them such as never and no. You may want your students to write two sentences on the backs of their activity strips that contain two double negatives such as: never, no; don't, none; won't, no; shouldn't none; couldn't, no; etc. Have each student exchange his/her work with another student. Direct the other student to rewrite the sentence correctly.

Topics Grammar/Usage
Subject/Verb Agreement, Double Negatives

Permission granted to copy student pages for purchaser's class. It is unlawful to copy the teacher materials.
© GRØW Publications

DAILY WRITING 3

Name _____ © GRØW Publications 28

Authors are not satisfied with using everyday words if they can build a clearer picture in the reader's mind by choosing a better word. Rewrite each of these sentences to better describe what is happening in the picture.

The mouse is going down the slide.

The tiger was roaring.

DAILY WRITING 3

Name _____ 29

Choose one sentence from each group of three that brings a stronger picture to your mind.

- ○ I closed the door.
- ○ I slammed the door.
- ○ I shut the door.

- ○ I scrubbed my teeth.
- ○ I brushed my teeth.
- ○ I cleaned my teeth.

Write three sentences of your own about something you did today.

Then underline the action word in each of the 12 sentences.

- ○ He went up the hill.
- ○ He jogged up the hill.
- ○ He raced up the hill.

- ○ _____
- ○ _____
- ○ _____

© GRØW Publications

DAILY WRITING 3

Name _____ © GRØW Publications 30

Picture the students in your class playing at recess. Draw one student or a group of students. Use sentences to describe the scene.
Use strong verbs.

Teacher Notes - DAILY WRITING - Grade 3

Answers/Comments — 28

Student sentences will vary.
Motivate your students to write more than one sentence to describe each picture. If you notice students who have written a very descriptive passage, ask them to share with the class. Activities such as this can lead young writers into using descriptive scenes in their stories. Here are two examples you may want to use.
1. With tail flying and arms outstretched, my little mouse zipped happily down her new slide.
2. The tiger reared up on its hind legs. With jaws wide open and eyes burning, it roared like thunder at us.

Topics **Author's Craft**
Descriptive Language

Answers/Comments — 29

There are no correct answers although some of the verbs are obviously more descriptive than others. If your students have difficulty thinking of three sentences to write, allow them to just write two. Take the time to review the term <u>verb</u>. A verb is a word that expresses action or existence (state of being). Authors carefully choose the verbs they use in their stories. It is only through careful selection of words that a clear message can be communicated. Remind your students to be looking for strong verbs in their reading today and to use them in their writing.

Topics **Author's Craft**   **Parts of Speech**
Strong Verbs   Verb

Answers/Comments — 30

Student drawings and descriptions will vary. This is a follow-up exercise to Days 26 and 27. As your third graders begin to struggle less with the mechanics of writing, they can be encouraged to new challenges through awareness of the qualities of good writing. Immersing them in quality literature is a key to opening this door. Moreover, noticing attempts that are made and giving encouraging feedback are ways to move students towards writing and reading like accomplished authors.

Topics **Author's Craft**
Strong Verbs, Descriptive Language

Permission granted to copy student pages for purchaser's class. <u>It is unlawful</u> to copy the teacher materials.
© GRØW Publications

DAILY WRITING 3

Name _____ © GROW Publications   31

Many of these sentences run together. Decide where the capitals and ending marks (. ! ?) need to be so the story makes sense.

polar bears live in the frozen Arctic if they stand on their back legs they are tall enough to look an elephant in the eye the biggest polar bear ever measured stood 11 feet tall and weighed almost 1,000 pounds polar bears are strong swimmers they can swim 100 miles without stopping to rest

---

DAILY WRITING 3

Name _____ © GROW Publications   32

These two sisters are opposites. Describe what you think each one would be like by filling in the missing phrases. Underline the opposite words for each number.

SISTER 1	SISTER 2
1. likes to do quiet things	1. likes to do _____
2. talks in a soft voice	2. _____
3. _____	3. runs everywhere she goes
4. _____	4. likes hard work
5. _____	5. likes to be outside

DAILY WRITING 3

Name _____ © GROW Publications   33

Circle the correct spelling of the underlined words. Use a dictionary if you need to.

I like to <u>right</u> <u>write</u> about animals. I <u>wait</u> <u>weight</u> until I find a special <u>won</u> <u>one</u>. I usually <u>see</u> <u>sea</u> them in books or in movies. Then I <u>read</u> <u>reed</u> about them in books and magazines. I often watch a video I've <u>heard</u> <u>herd</u> about that tells me more. When I have <u>read</u> <u>red</u> and <u>scene</u> <u>seen</u> all kinds of information I start to <u>write</u> <u>rite</u>. I'm never <u>bored</u> <u>board</u>.

Teacher Notes - DAILY WRITING - Grade 3

Answers/Comments — 31

Polar; Arctic. If; eye. The; pounds. Polar; swimmers. They; rest.
Throughout the *Daily Writing* activities, the importance of students using punctuation marks and capitals as they write has been stressed. It is only through continual practice that these conventions go through the stages of approximation to automaticity (being able to use them automatically as they write). Editing is the cleaning up of a piece of writing, catching the few things the writer may have missed while drafting. It is the preparation of a piece of writing for a larger audience.

Topics

Writing Process	Sentences
Proofreading/Editing	Structure
Punctuation, Capitalization	Run-on Sentences

Answers/Comments — 32

Student responses should show an understanding of the concepts.
1. likes to do loud things; 2. talks in a loud voice; 3. walks everywhere she goes; 4. likes easy work or hates hard work; 5. likes to be inside or hates to be outside
Authors often use opposite qualities in characters to build a contrast. <u>Big Sister, Little Sister</u> by Charlotte Zolotow; <u>Big Dog, Little Dog</u> by P.D. Eastman and <u>Kevin's Grandma</u> by Judith Viorst, are examples of literature books that establish clear contrasts. Share examples of the use of opposites and direct your students to use this style in one of their pieces of writing.

Topics

Grammar/Usage
Antonyms

Answers/Comments — 33

Correct responses should include: write, wait, one, see, read, heard, read, seen, write, bored. The homophones in this paragraph are words that sound (phone) the same (homo) but are spelled differently. It may be helpful if your students contribute to a homophone book or chart that they can use as a reference.

Topics

Grammar/Usage
Homophones/Homographs

Permission granted to copy student pages for purchaser's class. It is unlawful to copy the teacher materials.
© GROW Publications

Daily Writing 3

Name _____ © GRØW Publications   34

Choose a word from each group. Cross out the others. Write a sentence using your choice.

tail
tale

flower
flour

our
hour

their   there
    they're

Daily Writing 3

Name _____ © GRØW Publications   35

Match the word with its definition.

singular   more than one

plural   a word that means a person, place, or thing

noun   one

Place an **X** in the box(es) that describe each word.

WORD	Singular	Plural	Noun
wheel			
lunches			
school			
deer			
trees			

Daily Writing 3

Name _____ © GRØW Publications   36

In this story <u>New Shoes</u>, cross out information not needed and add information using carets (^) so it makes more sense.

When you see my new shoes, you'll want so some just them. They are awesome! When I found them, my mom said, "Yes they are really different." My little couldn't quit staring at them. He was speechless. When went out of the store, everyone stared at feet. I could tell they were dying to have some new just like me mine.

Teacher Notes - DAILY WRITING - Grade 3

Answers/Comments — 34

Student sentences will vary. This activity is a follow-up to Activity 33. The homophones their, there and they're are difficult ones for third graders to keep straight. Instead or working on all three at once, begin with just one of them until your students know how to use it automatically as they write. Then move on to the next one. This strategy also works for other homophones such as two, too and to.

Topics Grammar/Usage
Homophones/Homographs

Answers/Comments — 35

singular-one; plural-more than one; noun-a word that means a person, place or thing. wheel - S, N; lunches - P, N; school - S, N; deer - S, P, N; trees - P, N.
Review the definition of a noun. It is a word that stands for a person, place or thing. There are many rules for adding plurals to words. You may have some students ready for this extra information. Some of the most common ones are:
* Most nouns - add s
* Words ending in a consonant followed by y - add es
* Words ending in a vowel followed by y - add s

Topics Parts of Speech
Noun
Common Noun, Singular and Plural Nouns

Answers/Comments — 36

Student revisions will vary. ~~so~~; just ^like them; little^brother, cousin, friend, etc.; when ^I went; at ^my feet; new ^shoes just; ~~me~~ In this short story, your students were asked to cross out or add a word. They should be familiar with this type of revision strategy from previous lessons. Remind your students that, as they revise, they need to think of the person who will be reading their stories. The ultimate goal is for students to revise with "the shadow of a reader" peeking over their shoulders. In their minds, they will be asking these questions: Will they understand? What else should I add? Do I need all of this?

Topics Writing Process
Revising
Story Makes Sense, Revision Strategies

Permission granted to copy student pages for purchaser's class. It is unlawful to copy the teacher materials.
© GRØW Publications

DAILY WRITING 3

Name _____ © GROW Publications 37

This story needs more information. Write two sentences on the lines. Then decide where they should go by putting a ★ and a ■ where you want the sentences to go in the story.

The Pignic ★

My mom said, "We're going on a picnic."

I said, "Can I take Wilbur?"

I decided to take him ■ anyway.

Was my mom ever surprised!

DAILY WRITING 3

Name _____ © GROW Publications 38

Write an ending to this story.

The Perfect Day - Almost

The sun's rays beat down on the water. It was the warmest day of the year but I hardly even noticed. I was having the perfect day. I floated in the water like a cloud floats in the sky sipping my cool drink. What a life!

DAILY WRITING 3

Name _____ 39

Why do you think stories have titles?

Write four good titles from books you have read, stories you have heard, or stories you have written.

© GROW Publications

Teacher Notes - DAILY WRITING - Grade 3

Answers/Comments [37]

Student sentences will vary. Carets are best used for adding words, phrases or short sentences. When your students need to add a large amount of information to their stories, it is much easier for them to choose a symbol, write the additional information on the margin or back of their paper or on another sheet, and use the chosen symbol to mark its placement in the story. This activity emphasizes this skill.

Topics
Writing Process	Writing Process
Drafting	Revising
Topics Developed with Details	Revision Strategies

Answers/Comments [38]

Student endings to this story will vary. Your class may need to use the back of their activity strips or separate pieces of paper to finish their stories. If there is time, allow them to share their stories with a partner. A good ending is a challenge to write. An ending lets you know a story is over. The author doesn't need to put "The End" because the reader should know the story is over. Endings may be surprising, show feelings, leave the reader wondering, or solve a problem. Connect this activity to reading by asking students to search for good endings in their reading, and pointing out or reading ones good examples.

Topics
Author's Craft
Creative Endings

Answers/Comments [39]

Answers to the question "Why do you think stories have titles?" may include:
* To capture the interest of a reader.
* To give the reader a hint of what is to come.
* To arouse curiosity.

Take this lesson a step further by having your students go to the library. Ask them to write down the titles of ten books with good titles and then ten books they would choose not to read because of the title.

Topics
Author's Craft
Titles

Permission granted to copy student pages for purchaser's class. It is unlawful to copy the teacher materials.
© GRØW Publications

DAILY WRITING 3

Name _____ © GROW Publications

40

Use your imagination to make up a character or think of someone you know. Use the map below to tell what this character is like.

CHARACTER'S NAME: _____

Looks like
_____
_____
_____
_____

Age: _____

Actions
_____

Things he/she says
_____

Interests/hobbies
_____
_____
_____
_____

DAILY WRITING 3

Name _____

41

Read each sentence and decide which part, if any, needs a capital letter. If <u>no</u> capital letters are missing, fill in the circle that goes with the word "None."

1. Tasha and i wrote the story.   None
   ○   ○   ○   ○

2. they want to leave after lunch.   None
   ○   ○   ○   ○

3. His mom will come back on tuesday.   None
   ○   ○   ○   ○   ○

4. Her Aunt pat lives in Wisconsin.   None
   ○   ○   ○   ○   ○

© GROW Publications

DAILY WRITING 3

Name _____

42

There are 3 types of sentences. Write an example of each one on the lines below.

THIS SENTENCE TELLS SOMETHING
_____
_____

THIS SENTENCE ASKS SOMETHING
_____
_____

THIS SENTENCE SHOWS STRONG FEELING
_____
_____

© GROW Publications

Teacher Notes - DAILY WRITING - Grade 3

Answers/Comments   40

Students' listed information will vary. Developing a story character can be a lot of fun. Tell your students that their characters can be a people or animals. It is often easier to write about a real person or an actual animal. Many authors base the characters in their stories on real people. An author such as Marc Brown has a character named Arthur who is really Marc Brown himself. Grandma Thora was based on his Grandma. Encourage your students to write a true or fiction story using the character they developed.

Topics

Writing Process	Author's Craft
Prewriting	Develops Story Characters
Mapping/Clustering	

Answers/Comments   41

1. Tasha and I; 2. They want; 3. on Tuesday 4. Pat lives
This type of activity includes a typical format often found in the language mechanics section of a standardized test. The format is often very confusing. Be sure to tell your students that each line is a complete sentence. Also, there is no reason for the position the slashes are placed between the groups of words. Sometimes it will be after one word, sometimes after three. Further their understanding by asking them to write two new sentences on the backs of their activity strips.

Topics **Mechanics**
Capitalization
Pronoun I, Beginning of Sentence, Proper Noun

Answers/Comments   42

Student sentences will vary. Remind your students to think carefully about which ending mark fits with each type of sentence. It may be enough for your students to know there are different types of sentences without attaching the more complicated labels. The three types of sentences in the exercise are declarative, interrogative and exclamatory. Similar to classifying words into parts of speech, this is the way whole sentences are classified in the English language. Have your students use a variety of sentence types in their writing each day.

Topics **Sentences**
Types
Declarative, Interrogative, Exclamatory

Permission granted to copy student pages for purchaser's class. It is unlawful to copy the teacher materials.
© GRØW Publications

DAILY WRITING 3

Name _____ © GROW Publications 43

Decide which punctuation mark, if any, is missing in each sentence. If one of the punctuation marks listed is needed, fill in the circle. If not, fill in the circle next to the word "None."

1. Is your dog nice   ○. ○, ○? ○! ○None
2. I miss my friend   ○. ○, ○? ○! ○None
3. What book are you reading now   ○. ○, ○? ○! ○None
4. I will take my book home with me. ○. ○, ○? ○! ○None
5. That car is going to hit us   ○. ○, ○? ○! ○None

DAILY WRITING 3

Name _____ © GROW Publications 44

Circle the 9 misspelled words in this story. Correct the misspelled words by rewriting each of them above the word. Use a dictionary if you need to.

<u>Wolves</u>   Wolves leive in groups. Thay are meat-eaters. Wolves will eat enything from a mouse to a moose. When a wolf pack hunts, the members of the pack werk together as a team. This makes it possible to hunt very larg anemals. Wolves are very interesting anemals. Thay are among the most intelligent anemals on earth.

DAILY WRITING 3

Name _____ © GROW Publications 45

This writer is planning a story about wolves. What is wrong with the plan?

History
* related to dogs tamed 12,000 years ago.

Baby Wolves
* best parents in world
* mom stays close for weeks
* born underground in den
* group called litter

Senses
* good hearing
* turn their ears to sound
* good sense of smell
* not good eyesight

Three Little Pigs and the Big Bad Wolf
* wolves like to eat pigs
* wolves huff and puff

Teacher Notes - DAILY WRITING - Grade 3

Answers/Comments | 43

1. ? (question mark); 2. . (period); 3. ? (question mark); 4. none 5. ! (exclamation mark). If your students finish quickly, ask them to answer this question on the backs of their activity strips: Why do authors use ending punctuation marks (.) (?) (!)? The following points should be reviewed:
1. To signal the end of a thought.
2. To show what type of sentence was used.
3. To tell the reader what tone of voice to use.
4. To better communicate his/her message.

Topics
Sentences
Types
Declarative, Interrogative, Exclamatory

Answers/Comments | 44

Answers: leive –> live, Thay –> They, enything –> anything, werk –> work, larg –> large, anemals –> animals, anemals –> animals, thay –> they, anemals –> animals. You may want your students to work in pairs on this exercise. This activity models a process for editing that students can use in editing their own writings. It may be easier for your students to use a colored pencil to circle words and correct them. It is important that students do not erase the misspelled words. It is only in looking at their misspellings that you can evaluate how close they are to actually spelling the word correctly.

Topics
Writing Process
Proofreading/Editing
Spelling

Answers/Comments | 45

Student answers should explain that all of the information is true except the part about the three little pigs. The focus is lost in the part about the three pigs. An author would not typically combine information in this way. Instruct your students to write their answers on the backs of their activity strips or on separate pieces of paper. Your students will be using the information on this activity to write leads for Activity 46.

Topics
Writing Process
Drafting
Focused Message

Permission granted to copy student pages for purchaser's class. It is unlawful to copy the teacher materials.
© GROW Publications

Daily Writing 3

Name _____ © GRØW Publications

46

Whatever you are writing, the beginning or **lead** is a very important part of the story. Use the information from Activity 45 to write two good leads for a nonfiction report about wolves.

Daily Writing 3

Name _____ © GRØW Publications

47

Complete the chart below by thinking of different stories you can write.

Stories about my life	Fiction stories I can write	Things I'd like to research	People to whom I'd like to write

---

Daily Writing 3

Name _____ © GRØW Publications

48

From Activity 47, choose a topic. Make a list of things you want to include in your story. If you **choose to** research something, write down what you already know.

Teacher Notes - DAILY WRITING - Grade 3

Answers/Comments | 46

Students' leads will vary. Remind your students to disregard the section in Activity 45 about the three pigs and the wolf. Review the purpose of a lead with your class. The lead or beginning "hooks the reader" and makes him or her want to read on. Leads in nonfiction animal writing often start with a brief description of the animal in its habitat, an unusual fact the author has chosen, or the author's opinion of the animal. You may want to use this lead as an example:
"Wolves are among the most intelligent animals on earth." (opinion)

Topics
Author's Craft
Creative Leads

Answers/Comments | 47

Student responses will vary. Completing a task like this one helps you to assess your students' abilities to choose topics. Some students may sit the entire time and generate two ideas. This lets you know that lessons in topic selection are needed. Share differing ways in which topics can be chosen. These may include: Observing what is happening around you, reading a book and getting an idea or writing something you want to remember. Your students will need their charts for activity 48.

Topics
Writing Process
Prewriting
Topic Selection

Student/Teacher Assessment
Student and Teacher Assessment

Answers/Comments | 48

Student responses will vary. Your class may need to use the backs of their activity sheets or separate pieces of paper to record their information. This is an important part of the writing process. Planning for writing helps a writer retrieve known information. It is a way of brainstorming with yourself. As your students become more sophisticated in their writings, they will plan their stories using carefully selected, important details. You may want your students to continue their stories during writing time.

Topics
Writing Process
Prewriting
Brainstorming

Permission granted to copy student pages for purchaser's class. It is unlawful to copy the teacher materials.
© GRØW Publications

DAILY WRITING 3

Name _____ © GROW Publications 49

Place the quotation ("talk") marks where they belong.

Mom, can I have a candy bar? asked Sarah.
No, not today, said Mom.
Mom, can I have some gum? asked Sarah.
No, maybe next time, said Mom.
Mom, can I have some ice cream? asked Sarah.
No, it will melt today. What are you doing? asked Mom.
I'm writing my list for next time, said Sarah smiling.

DAILY WRITING 3

Name _____ © GROW Publications 50

The capital letters are missing in this conversation. Circle the letters that need to be capitalized and write the correct letter above the circle.

"i know we're going to be late," said nicky
"what took you so long?" asked rachel.
"do you see my hair?" asked michael.
"yes, i sure do," said nicky.
"it looks very interesting," said rachel.
"i spent hours on it this morning," said michael.
"no wonder you're late," said rachel.

DAILY WRITING 3

Name _____ 51

Add the missing punctuation marks to this conversation.

" I still need some peanut butter " said Anton

" No, stop " said the store owner

" My mom said to get some peanut butter " I said as I pulled the jar off the shelf

The store owner said " Let's get out of here "

" Oh no " I said running after her

© GROW Publications

Teacher Notes - DAILY WRITING - Grade 3

Answers/Comments | 49

"Mom,...bar?" asked Sarah. "No,...today," said Mom.
"Mom,...gum?" asked Sarah. "No,...time," said Mom.
"Mom,...cream?" asked Sarah. "No,...doing?" asked Mom.
"I'm...time," said Sarah smiling.

Quotation marks enclose the words of the speaker, including the needed ending punctuation mark. They are important because they signal the reader that someone is talking. Have your students use conversation in the stories they are writing today.

Topics
Mechanics
Punctuation
Quotation Mark

Answers/Comments | 50

"<u>I</u> know...said <u>N</u>icky.   "<u>W</u>hat took...asked <u>R</u>achel.
"<u>D</u>o you...asked <u>M</u>ichael.   "<u>Y</u>es, I know...said <u>N</u>icky.
"<u>I</u>t looks...said <u>R</u>achel.   "<u>I</u> spent...said <u>M</u>ichael.
"<u>N</u>o wonder...said <u>R</u>achel.

This activity provides additional practice with the mechanics of dialogue. In a follow-up discussion, ask your students to compare how these sentences are capitalized to how regular sentences are capitalized. They will find no difference as far as capitalizing the beginning word in the sentence and proper nouns.

Topics
Writing Process	Mechanics
Proofreading/Editing	Capitalization
Capitalization	Direct Quote

Answers/Comments | 51

* "I still need some peanut butter," said Anton.
* "No, stop! (or ,)" said the store owner.
* "My mom said to get some peanut butter," I said as I pulled the jar off the shelf.
* The store owner said, "Let's get out of here!"
* "Oh no! (or ,) " I said running after her.

Punctuating conversation can be difficult for students. The more practice they can have, the less complicated it will seem to them.

Topics
Writing Process	Mechanics
Proofreading/Editing	Capitalization
Punctuation	Direct Quote

Permission granted to copy student pages for purchaser's class. It is unlawful to copy the teacher materials.
© GRØW Publications

DAILY WRITING 3

Name _____ © GROW Publications 52

Write a short conversation between yourself and another person. Be sure to include the speakers' names.

DAILY WRITING 3

Name _____ © GROW Publications 53

Read the stories in the boxes and answer the questions below.

Lassie is a good dog. Lassie does everything I tell her. Lassie sits, stays and rolls over. I throw balls to Lassie and Lassie brings them back to me. Lassie is the best dog in the world.	Dogs make wonderful pets. Dogs can be trained to do many things. Some dogs help blind people and other dogs work with the police. Dogs have been called a person's best friend.

What is wrong with these stories? .... Change words in each story so it sounds better.

DAILY WRITING 3

Name _____ © GROW Publications 54

Choose one word from each pair. Circle your choices. Write a short story using those four words.

found - discovered

hurried - rushed

noise - uproar

angry - furious

Teacher Notes - DAILY WRITING - Grade 3

Answers/Comments | 52

Students' conversation writings will vary. You may need to model one or two lines for your class. Think aloud your use of quotation marks and how you always designate who is speaking. Even though students are told not to use the same words over and over again, "said" is an exception to this rule. Readers do not really notice the word said in conversations. Ask for volunteers to share interesting conversations they have written with the rest of the class. Can the class tell what each of the characters is like by the conversation that took place?

Topics
Mechanics
Punctuation
Quotation Mark

Author's Craft
Dialogue

Answers/Comments | 53

The writer repeats the words Lassie and dogs a number of times.
Ask your students to fix the words that have been repeated by crossing them out and putting a word that sounds better above the word. The words he, she, they, them, etc., are pronouns. Pronouns can take the place of nouns, and make writing and speaking sound more realistic. Make sure students are aware of both singular and plural pronouns such as the following:
  Singular Pronouns - I, you, she, he, it, me, her, him
  Plural Pronouns - we, you, they, us, them

Topics
Parts of Speech
Pronoun

Answers/Comments | 54

The short stories that students compose will vary.
Allow your students to work in pairs to complete this activity, and they may need to use the backs of their activity strips or separate pieces of paper if they run out of room. To give your students an audience for their writing, ask for volunteers to share with the whole class or direct two sets of partners to share with each other. Underscore that synonyms are an important writer's tool. They are words that mean the same or about the same thing. Authors carefully choose words to express the meaning which they are trying to convey.

Topics
Grammar/Usage
Synonyms

Permission granted to copy student pages for purchaser's class. It is unlawful to copy the teacher materials.
© GRØW Publications

Daily Writing 3

Name _____ © GRØW Publications

55

Notice how the sentence below has been moved so that the passage makes better sense. Draw a different arrow to a place where the sentence would sound even better.

Zebras

Zebras are one of the only true wild horses left in the world. Like all horses, they have long handsome faces with big gentle eyes. /All horses belong to the animal group with the scientific name Equus (EE-kwis)./ They also have strong bodies and long, slender legs. ◂

✂ ══

Daily Writing 3

Name _____ © GRØW Publications

56

Circle the sentence that is out of place. Draw an arrow to the place you think it should go.

Bear for Sale

Would you like to buy a cute bear? It will only cost you $1.00. Most bears are just fuzzy and cute. So, get your dollar and take home your new best friend. This bear is fuzzy, cute and soft as a marshmallow.

✂ ══

Daily Writing 3

Name _____ © GRØW Publications

57

Think of one thing that you did or that happened to you. The questions in the box may give you some ideas. Write what you think of on the line. Then, draw a picture of the beginning, middle, and end of your story.

Where have I gone?	Has anyone gotten hurt?
Who have I visited?	What games have I played?
What did I do that was fun?	What happened at school?

....

BEGINNING	MIDDLE	END

Teacher Notes - DAILY WRITING - Grade 3

Answers/Comments [55]

The noted sentence should be the second one in the passage. This revision strategy helps a student learn how to move information from place to place without recopying the entire piece of writing. Be sure to use the available technology in your school to demonstrate how this same task is completed on the computer by cutting and pasting. Consider having your students experiment using this strategy in their writing lesson today.

Topics Writing Process
Revising
Revision Strategies

Answers/Comments [56]

The sentence "So get your dollar and take home your new best friend," should be circled and moved to the end of the story.
In this exercise, your your class is able to practice the revision strategy they were utilizing in Activity 55. Be sure your students understand that they can use this strategy to move words, ideas, and sentences around in their writing.

Topics Writing Process
Revising
Revision Strategies

Answers/Comments [57]

Students' work on this exercise will vary. Choosing a topic is often difficult for some students. If students are able to ask themselves questions like the ones in the box, they will be able to choose topics more easily. Drawing the beginning, middle, and end of the story is a way to record the sequence of events that forms the basic structure of a story about something that has happened. Allow your students to continue writing their stories during your regular writing time.

Topics	Writing Process	Writing Process	Author's Craft
	Prewriting	Drafting	Organizational Pattern
	Topic Selection	Organized Structure	Beginning, Middle, End

Permission granted to copy student pages for purchaser's class. It is unlawful to copy the teacher materials.
© GRØW Publications

Daily Writing 3

Name _____ © GRØW Publications

58

Help this student make his news report sound more like the way people should talk. Circle each word that needs to be changed and write the correct word above it.

Passport Around the World Day

We got a special day at our school. The students loves it. Every teacher choosed a different country for the class to study. Then, on Passport Day, we goed to three different countries. We really learns a lot.

Daily Writing 3

Name _____ © GRØW Publications

59

When authors compare one thing to another, it helps a story come alive. Choose one of the comparisons in the list. Write a short story using your choice.

as quiet as a butterfly
   eyes like stars
   eats like a pig
   slept like a log

Daily Writing 3

Name _____ © GRØW Publications

60

Choose one of the two pictures. **X** the one you choose. Write three sentences about that picture. End the first sentence with a question mark, the second with a period, and the third with an exclamation point.

Teacher Notes - DAILY WRITING - Grade 3

Answers/Comments — 58

We **have** a special day at our school. The students **love** it. Every teacher **chooses** a different country for the class to study. Then, on Passport Day, we **go** to three different countries. We really **learn** a lot.

If necessary, give your students a hint by telling them that there are five words to look for, and there is one such word in each sentence.

Topics
Writing Process
Proofreading/Editing
Standard Grammar

Answers/Comments — 59

Students' short stories will vary.
Comparisons using the words like or as are called **similes**. Your students do not need to remember the term. It is important for them to realize that comparing one thing to another is a way for the author to help the reader get a clearer picture of what is happening in the story. Poetry is filled with comparisons. Be alert to stories and poems where comparisons are used so you can focus your students' attention on one of the qualities of good writing.

Topics
Author's Craft
Figurative Language

Answers/Comments — 60

Student sentences will vary. Each sentence must conclude with a different punctuation mark.
This warm-up lesson will help you determine if your students know the terms for the ending punctuation marks. If students finish early, ask them to write three more sentences on the backs of their activity strips about the other picture. Discuss with your class the importance of using the proper punctuation. It tells the reader what kind of voice to use when reading a sentence, and helps the reader better understand the author's message.

Topics
Mechanics
Punctuation
End of Sentence (. ! ?)

Permission granted to copy student pages for purchaser's class. It is unlawful to copy the teacher materials.
© GRØW Publications

DAILY WRITING 3

Name _____ © GRØW Publications 61

A **noun** is a _____, place, or _____.
An **adjective** helps describe a noun. For example:

adjective → **black**   noun → **hair**
adjective → **messy**   noun → **desk**
adjective → **bright** noun → **light**

Think of an adjective to go with each of the nouns below.

_____ frog   _____ slide   _____ paper

_____ book   _____ ball   _____ shoes

DAILY WRITING 3

Name _____ © GRØW Publications 62

This writer is planning a fiction story. Finish the plan with ideas you have.

Setting — When? _____
           — Where? _____

——————————— **Characters** ———————————

Problem Money is missing.

Solution _____

DAILY WRITING 3

Name _____ © GRØW Publications 63

Choose one of your characters from Activity 62, and tell what that character is like. Give lots of details. The words in the box may help you think of ideas.

looks like	does
unusual habits	
says	interests
age	name	home

Teacher Notes - DAILY WRITING - Grade 3

Answers/Comments — 61

person, thing   Students' choice of adjectives will vary.
Introduce your students to the term <u>adjective</u>. Many of them have probably been using adjectives in their daily writing. Try and find a story or two that your students have written that contain adjectives. See if your students can pick them out as you read. When adjectives are used in a story, they help a reader build a better picture of what the author is saying. For example:
- I have a dog.
- I have a large, brown and white St. Bernard.

Topics
Parts of Speech
Adjective

Answers/Comments — 62

Students' work will vary.
Unlike personal narrative or nonfiction stories, fiction stories cannot be planned using a list or a web. In a typical fiction story, there is a problem that needs to be solved. To illustrate this point, you may want to read some picture books such as Don and Audrey Wood's <u>King and Bidgood's in the Bathtub</u> or Helen Lester's <u>Tacky the Penguin</u>. Encourage your students to use a story map like the one in the exercise to plan their fiction stories. Your students will be using the map they developed in Activity 63.

Topics
Author's Craft
Organizational Pattern
Problem, Events, Solution

Answers/Comments — 63

Students' character descriptions will vary.
Tell students to use words or phrases to develop their characters. This type of activity can be used to develop characters that are made up and characters that are real. Extend this warm-up lesson by asking each of your students to write a conversation between his/her character and another person. Through the conversation, the reader should be able to tell what the character is like.

Topics
Author's Craft
Develops Story Characters

Permission granted to copy student pages for purchaser's class. <u>It is unlawful</u> to copy the teacher materials.
© GRØW Publications

Daily Writing 3

Name _____ © GRØW Publications 64

Read the sentences in the paragraph. Add the correct punctuation marks. Circle the letters that need to be capitalized and write the correct letters above them.

i looked down the long hill it was a long way down lets go i said to my brother off we went the air rushed around us What a ride

---

Daily Writing 3

Name _____ © GRØW Publications 65

Make a list of all the places you know where you need to write capital letters.

A B C

Daily Writing 3

Name _____ © GRØW Publications 66

See if you can find 11 words that need to start with a capital letter. Circle the letter and write the corrected letter above it.

december 10, 1996

dear david,

    i am so glad you came to visit us last thursday. we always have fun going to the museum in denver. i hope you can come again in january.

    your friend,

    chris

Teacher Notes - DAILY WRITING - Grade 3

Answers/Comments — 64

<u>I</u> looked down the long hill<u>.</u> <u>I</u>t was a long way down<u>.</u> "<u>L</u>et<u>'</u>s go<u>."</u> I said to my brother<u>.</u> <u>O</u>ff we went<u>.</u> <u>T</u>he air rushed around u<u>s</u>. What a ride<u>!</u>

Don't be surprised if many of your students incorrectly punctuate the sentence that needs quotation marks. It is a difficult skill and they have just recently been introduced to it.

Topics
Mechanics
Capitalization
Pronoun I, Beginning of Sentence, Direct Quote

Answers/Comments — 65

Students' work should demonstrate that they know some of the times when capitals should be used. Through their classroom instruction, your students should know that the following words need to be capitalized:
1. beginning of a sentence
2. people's names
3. month, days
4. cities, states
5. greeting and closing of a letter

Topics
Mechanics
Capitalization
Proper noun

Answers/Comments — 66

<u>D</u>ecember; <u>D</u>ear <u>D</u>avid; <u>I</u>; <u>T</u>hursday; <u>W</u>e; <u>D</u>enver; <u>I</u>; <u>J</u>anuary; <u>Y</u>our; <u>C</u>hris

Once your students know which words need to be capitalized, they should be expected to use capitals at the beginning of these words as they are writing their drafts. The only way for students to begin to use their skills in their writing automatically is to practice using them every day.

Topics
Mechanics
Capitalization
Pronoun I, Proper Noun

Permission granted to copy student pages for purchaser's class. It is unlawful to copy the teacher materials.
© GRØW Publications

DAILY WRITING 3

Name _____ © GRØW Publications

67

A **noun** is a person, place or thing.

A **proper noun** is a certain person, place, or thing.

Choose a proper noun to go with each of the nouns below. Use the proper nouns to write about your school on a separate piece of paper.

noun	proper noun	noun	proper noun
teacher	your teacher _____	state	your state _____
school	your school _____	month	this month _____
city	your city _____	day	this day _____

DAILY WRITING 3

Name _____ © GRØW Publications

68

The author reread this story and found there were 2 missing sentences. Choose a symbol for each sentence and add them to the story.

☐ In other words, I'm the boss.

☐ I have to guard my space with an eagle's eye.

Queen of the House

I'm B.J. the cat and I'm queen of the house. I tell the dog what to do, the cat what to do, and the family what to do.

I live in Sarah's bedroom. Whenever the dog or other cat tries to come in, I arch my back and "hiss" at them. They get the message. You should see them turn tail and tear out of there.

DAILY WRITING 3

Name _____ © GRØW Publications

69

Use the words in the box to make 4 compound words. Write a short story using 2 or more of the words you made.

fall	snow	ball
foot	shine	basket
sun	yard	back

1 _____
2 _____
3 _____
4 _____

Teacher Notes - DAILY WRITING - Grade 3

Answers/Comments | 67

Students' choice of proper nouns will vary. Review, with your students, the importance of capitalizing proper nouns. The capital letter is a signal to the reader that a spcific detail is being given such as a person's name, a particular place, etc. You may or may not wish to hold your students responsible for the term <u>proper noun</u>. They do need to know that in the English language, words that name a particular person, place, or thing fit together in a group.

Topics
Parts of Speech
Noun
Proper Noun

Answers/Comments | 68

The first sentence should be inserted at the end of the first paragraph. The second sentence should become the second sentence of the second paragraph.
Take this opportunity to discuss, with your students, the reasons for revision. Possibilities include: so the story will make sense, to add details or description, to give the reader a better picture of what is happening, to get rid of unneeded information. Using symbols such as * or ±, helps writers have the option of adding more than just a word or phrase. It doesn't matter what symbol they use.

Topics
Writing Process
Revising
Revision strategies

Answers/Comments | 69

football, snowfall, backyard, sunshine, basketball and backyard.
If your students need more writing room, ask them to finish their stories on the backs of the activity strips or have them write their stories on separate pieces of paper. Compound words are two words that are joined together, and do not always join the meanings of the two words used. For example, brainstorm and pigtail.

Topics
Grammar/Usage
Compound Words

Permission granted to copy student pages for purchaser's class. <u>It is unlawful</u> to copy the teacher materials.
© GRØW Publications

DAILY WRITING 3

Name _____ © GROW Publications **70**

<u>Dog's house</u> means that the _____ owns the _____.

Dog's is a possessive. What is the punctuation mark called that is used by a writer to show possession?

_____

Think of something that someone in your family or a friend owns. Write the two words in the blanks below. Write a short story to tell more about what you chose.

_____ _____
PERSON   **THING**

DAILY WRITING 3

Name _____ **71**

A **paragraph** is a group of sentences about one idea. Look at the shape of the paragraph below. Tell everything you notice about it on the lines.

> Every person's fingerprints are different. This makes fingerprinting a good tool for the police. They can use fingerprints to show that a person touched an object.

_____
_____
_____
_____
_____
_____

DAILY WRITING 3

© GROW Publications

Name _____ **72**

A **paragraph** is a of group sentences about one thing or the words of one speaker. Add two more paragraphs to this conversation.

"You know what Mom would say about that. It's dangerous coming down that hill," said Anthony.

"Where do you want to go?" asked Anthony.

"Let's go over past the pond and go up White's Hill," said David.

Teacher Notes - DAILY WRITING - Grade 3

Answers/Comments — 70

Students' short stories will vary. Instruct each student to write (or continue) their short story on the back of his/her activity strip or on a separate piece of paper. Be sure they understand that they need to include their possessive in their stories. Students seem to acquire this skill through practice. They should be expected to use it in the editing stage of the writing process, although some students may be using it while drafting. This usually means they can use it automatically.

Topics
Mechanics
Punctuation
Apostrophe

Parts of Speech
Noun
Possessive Noun

Answers/Comments — 71

Discuss your students' answers. They may include: shaped like a school bus, first line pushed in, all about one thing, etc.
Introduce your students to the term <u>paragraphs</u>, or reinforce this word as necessary. Ask the class to look in books they have at their desks or show them how a book has been divided into paragraphs. The purpose of paragraphs is to signal the reader that the idea, time, place or speaker is changing. The school bus shape helps the students to remember that the first line is pushed in or indented.

Topics
Mechanics
Paragraphing
Indenting, Paragraph Structure

Answers/Comments — 72

Student paragraphs will vary.
When students are first introduced to paragraphing in third grade, some are ready to use the information in their writing and others are still struggling with correctly punctuating their sentences. If students are ready for this step, expect it of them. If not, use your individual editing conferences to discuss how a student would use paragraphing in his/her own story.

Topics
Mechanics
Paragraphing
Indenting, Paragraph Structure

Permission granted to copy student pages for purchaser's class. <u>It is unlawful</u> to copy the teacher materials.
© GRØW Publications

DAILY WRITING 3

Name _____ © GRØW Publications   73

You indent and start a new paragraph when you change: **ideas, time, place, speaker**

Add a paragraph to the two below. Change the time or place.

    My brother and I flew down the hill on our sleds. My brother's favorite thing to do is sledding. Today we decided to go down Hurricane Hill.

    All of a sudden, I saw my brother's sled heading for a big tree. I froze in fear. At the last minute, he bailed out.

DAILY WRITING 3

Name _____ © GRØW Publications   74

Add verbs (action words) to this paragraph. Remember, strong verbs are the engine of the sentence. They help the story move forward.

    One icy cold night, we decided to warm up our house so my dad _____ a fire in the fireplace. Within minutes, smoke was _____ into the family room. Dad _____ out the fire.

    The next day he _____ up the chimney to see what had happened. He _____ the problem.

DAILY WRITING 3

Name _____   75

Make a list of all 5 places where commas are used in this letter.

January 23, 1997

Dear Jennifer,
    We're going to be in Lead, South Dakota this summer. We hope to see Mt. Rushmore, Bear Country, the Flintstone Village, and you.
    I'm really excited.
               Love,
               Sarah

1. _____
2. _____
3. _____
4. _____
5. _____

© GRØW Publications

Teacher Notes - DAILY WRITING - Grade 3

Answers/Comments [73]

Student paragraphs will vary.
Discuss with the class the reason why the second paragraph was indented. In this case, there was a change of idea. It is important for your students to learn these four reasons why new paragraphs are formed (change of idea, time, place, speaker). Students can then think when they are writing, "Oh, I just changed place, I need to make a new paragraph," etc.

Topics
Mechanics
Paragraphing
Indenting

Answers/Comments [74]

Answers may include: started, lit; pouring, billowing; put, stamped; climbed, squeezed; discovered, identified.
If your students finish quickly, instruct each student to write a paragraph on the back of their activity strip about what dad discovered., reminding them to use strong verbs in their paragraphs. Take this opportunity to mention that verbs are not only action words but also show state of being (is, was, were, etc.). Be looking for strong verbs in students' pieces of writing so they can share them with the rest of the class.

Topics
Author's Craft
Strong Verbs

Answers/Comments [75]

Between a date and a year, between a city and state, commas in the series, and the greeting and closing of a letter.

Students may be able to name several more places commas are needed in writing. Remind the class that commas give the reader a signal to pause. Extend this activity by asking your students to write a letter to someone they know.

Topics

Mechanics	**Mechanics**
Capitalization	Punctuation
Greeting and Closing of a Letter	Comma

Permission granted to copy student pages for purchaser's class. It is unlawful to copy the teacher materials.
© GROW Publications

DAILY WRITING 3

Name _____ © GROW Publications

76

Choose a topic that you are interested in learning more about. Fill in the two charts below.

What I know	TOPIC: _____	What questions I have
_____		_____
_____		_____
_____		_____
_____		_____

DAILY WRITING 3

Name _____ © GROW Publications

77

Read the following paragraph. On the lines, write words or short phrases that will help you to remember the details in the paragraph.

Hummingbirds

Hummingbirds are the world's smallest birds. They are also the world's best fliers. One of the reasons is because of the size of their chest muscles. A lot of a hummingbird's weight is in its chest muscles. They can out-fly other birds a hundred times their size.

DAILY WRITING 3

Name _____

78

Practice your note-taking skills by writing words or short phrases on the lines to help you remember the details in the paragraph.

On the wing of the hummingbird there are ten main feathers. When its wings flap, these feathers vibrate. That's what makes the humming sound. Hummingbirds fly like little helicopters. They can fly in one spot, move side to side, go straight up, straight down, and even backwards. To take off, they just flap their wings and off they go.

Teacher Notes - DAILY WRITING - Grade 3

Answers/Comments — 76

Students' choice of topics and questions will vary.
Lifelong learners are continually asking themselves questions, wanting to know more about the world around them. One of our classroom goals should be to encourage curiosity and give students the skills to find answers to their questions. Using the type of strategy found in this warm-up lesson during prewriting, helps students retrieve what they know and gives them a focus for their research.

Topics Writing Process
Prewriting
Brainstorming

Answers/Comments — 77

Students' answers may include: world's smallest birds, best fliers, chest muscles are 1/3 of the bird's weight, can out fly-birds 100 times its size.
Note-taking is an important skill to learn. When students read information about a topic for the purpose of writing a report, note-taking helps them record important pieces of information. In this way they aren't copying from the author of the text they are reading; instead, they are compiling information from a variety of sources to write a report in their own voice and style.

Topics Writing Process
Prewriting
Note-taking

Answers/Comments — 78

Students should pick out important details from this selection, including things such as: have ten feathers, feathers vibrate, etc.
When students are working on research, take time to explore the structure of nonfiction books, reports, etc., with them. For example, if a student reads several zoo books, he/she will discover they are all set up in a similar way, covering description, habitat, food, interesting information, what they do, their young and their future. Once students realize what kind of information is available, it helps them develop questions about a topic, allowing the topic to have greater focus.

Topics Writing Process
Prewriting
Note-taking

Permission granted to copy student pages for purchaser's class. It is unlawful to copy the teacher materials.
© GRØW Publications

Daily Writing 3

Name _____ © GRØW Publications 79

Use the notes on the paper below to write your own paragraph about the hummingbird.

- spends a lot of time eating
- needs energy to fly and keep body warm
- eats a lot of sugar
- gathers sugar from nectar in flowers
- eats insects to get protein for muscles

Daily Writing 3

Name _____ © GRØW Publications 80

Fill in the circle of the line that has the correct punctuation.

(6) **Dear Phil** **Oct. 20 1996** (5)

We really had a good time in **Billings Montana**. The mountains are beautiful!
(7)
    Your penpal
(8) **Matthew**

5. ○ oct. 20, 1996
   ○ Octo. 20, 1996
   ○ Oct. 20, 1996
   ○ Correct as is.

6. ○ Dear Phil,
   ○ dear Phil,
   ○ Dear phil,
   ○ Correct as is.

7. ○ Billings, montana
   ○ Billings Montana,
   ○ Billings, Montana
   ○ Correct as is.

8. ○ your penpal
   ○ Your penpal,
   ○ your penpal,
   ○ Correct as is.

Daily Writing 3

Name _____ 81

Think of someone who would enjoy getting a letter from you. Fill out the information on the lines to the right. Use it to set up your letter on a separate piece of paper.

_____ (date)
_____ (greeting)
Body
_____ (closing)
_____ (signature)

© GRØW Publications

Teacher Notes - DAILY WRITING - Grade 3

Answers/Comments | 79

Student paragraphs will vary.
This warm-up lesson provides your students with the opportunity to develop paragraphs in their own style and voice working from the notes provided. Motivate your students to write their paragraphs in an interesting way, and each paragraph should have at least three details from the list on the activity strip. They can use the back of the activity strips or additional pieces of paper if they more writing space is needed.

Topics
Writing Process
Drafting
Topics Developed with Details

Answers/Comments | 80

5. Oct. 20, 1996   6. Dear Phil,   7. Billings, Montana   8. Your penpal,
This is example of one of the more confusing formats your students will encounter on a standardized test. Unless third graders have worked with this format, it is hard to think that two sentences could be considered to be a letter. Take time to discuss not only the placement of commas, but also the format of a letter. This would also be an excellent time to review with the class the parts of a letter (date, greeting, body, closing and signature).

Topics
Mechanics	Mechanics
Capitalization	Punctuation
Greeting and Closing of a Letter	Comma

Answers/Comments | 81

Student letters will vary.
This exercise will help to remind your students about letter format. It is important for your students to realize that they have an audience. You may want your students to go through the editing process, make a final copy, and then send their letters home to be mailed.

Topics
Writing Process	Mechanics
Prewriting	Capitalization
Form Selection	Greeting and Closing of a Letter

Permission granted to copy student pages for purchaser's class. It is unlawful to copy the teacher materials.
© GRØW Publications

Daily Writing 3

Name _____ © GRØW Publications   82

Circle the words that are misspelled. Write the correct spelling above the circled word.

The bear went doun to toun. The boy showted, "Get owt of here!" The bear grouled at him and lumbered on doun the street. It spotted a hot dog stand and pushed it to the grownd. After gobbling up pownds of hot dogs, it fell asleep with a soft, satisfied sownd, "Groul, groul, groul."

Daily Writing 3

Name _____ © GRØW Publications   83

If you want to write about yourself, something that happened in your life or someone you know, you write a **personal narrative**. See how many stories about your life you can think of to complete the table below.

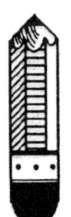

STORIES ABOUT ME	THINGS THAT HAPPENED	SOMEONE I KNOW

Daily Writing 3

Name _____   84

Choose one of your ideas from Activity 83. Fill in the web below to organize your ideas.

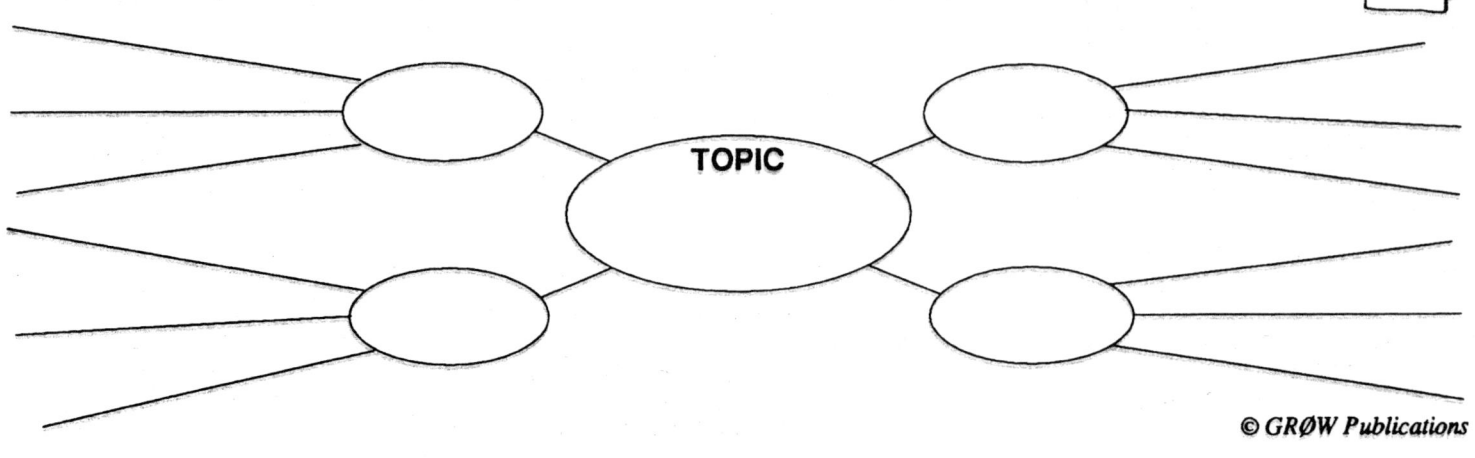

© GRØW Publications

Teacher Notes - DAILY WRITING - Grade 3

Answers/Comments — 82

down, town, shouted, out, growled, down, ground, pound, sound, growl, growl, growl

Ask your students what they noticed about the misspelled words. Comments may include: the "ou" words should have been "ow" and vice versa, both "ou" and "ow" make the same sound, etc.

Topics
Writing Process
Proofreading/Editing
Spelling

Answers/Comments — 83

The completed charts will vary. There are students who always have topics to write about, while other students may struggle when it is time to decide what to write next. After your students have completed thieir charts, you may want them to keep them in their writing notebooks or folders. Students who choose topics quickly, often have good self-questioning skills. For example, "What can I write about?" "Has anything happened recently?" "Who would it be fun to write about?" "What story do I need to write so I won't forget that time in my life?" Your students will need to use their charts again for Activity 84.

Topics
Writing Process
Prewriting
Topic Selection

Answers/Comments — 84

Webbing or clustering is a more organized brainstorming activity. You may want to model the use of a web for your students. These webs are needed for Activity 85. A sample of a student's work is shown below.

gray hair				telephone
glasses	**Looks Like**		**Hard of Hearing**	store
		<u>GREAT GRANDMA</u>		
kind	**Acts**		**Neat**	clothes
forgetful				hair

Topics
Writing Process
Prewriting
Mapping/Clustering

Permission granted to copy student pages for purchaser's class. <u>It is unlawful</u> to copy the teacher materials.
© GRØW Publications

Daily Writing 3

Name _____

85

Use your web from Activity 84 to write two different leads to your story. Think of where you want your story to start. Remember: some ideas for leads are **action, description, conversation, thinking in your head,** etc.

LEAD 1 _____
_____
_____

LEAD 2 _____
_____
_____

© GRØW Publications

Daily Writing 3

Name _____

86

Decide which ending to the short story works best. Check the box of your choice.

The Sneak

There she stood, a little black, shiny sneak. I knew she had done something wrong because, as usual, our dog was tattling on herself. If she's been a sneak while we're gone, she'll be waiting by the door with her ears flat to her head and a guilty look in her eyes. Sure enough, there was black hair and a warm spot on the couch. I scolded her, as usual.

ENDING 1 ☐
The next day when I came home there was no warm spot on the couch. It was on the bed. Oh, no!

ENDING 2 ☐
She listened politely, then walked away smiling.

© GRØW Publications

Daily Writing 3

Name _____

87

A sentence has two parts, the **subject** and the **predicate**.

SUBJECT: tells who or what the sentence is about.

PREDICATE: tells what the subject is or does.

Circle the subject and underline the predicate in the sentences below. Then write your own sentence and do the same thing.

1. (The dog) was a real sneak.
2. My desk is always neat.
3. The bear raided the picnic basket.

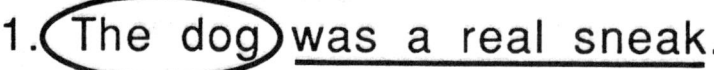

© GRØW Publications

Teacher Notes - DAILY WRITING - Grade 3

Answers/Comments — 85

Students' leads will vary. Authors, such as Roy Peter Clark in <u>Free to Write</u>, stress the importance of writing a creative lead. He says, " Through the lead, students can craft an opening passage that suggests an order for the rest of the story. The lead sharpens the focus and shares it with the reader." The lead can be what "hooks" the reader. It may answer the reader's most important question, "Why am I reading this?" Many of your students may choose to continue writing the story they have started in the past three activities. You may want them to choose their best lead and share it with the rest of the class.

Topics Author's Craft
Creative Leads

Answers/Comments — 86

Ending 1 is the most appropriate one for this story. If your students finish quickly, have them write a third ending on the reverse side of their activity strips. Ask your students which of the two endings they enjoyed more, and have students verbalize the reasons for their choices. Endings should seem just right but slightly surprise the reader. A writer should decide when he/she has said what they need to say and then stop. This would be a good time to focus on endings in both reading and writing.

Topics Author's Craft
Creative Endings

Answers/Comments — 87

2. My desk <u>**is always neat.**</u>
3. The bear <u>**raided the picnic basket.**</u>

Introduce (or review with) your students the terms <u>subject</u> and <u>predicate</u>. Both parts are needed to write a complete sentence. If your students are participating in standardized testing this year, they will need this information. If students complete this activity early, ask them to write three or four additional sentences on the back of their activity strips.

Topics Sentences
Parts
Subject, Predicate

Permission granted to copy student pages for purchaser's class. <u>It is unlawful</u> to copy the teacher materials.
© GRØW Publications

DAILY WRITING 3

Name _____ © GRØW Publications 88

Choose one of the sets of words. Circle your choice. Write a short story using the set of words you chose.

PAST
played
ran
rode

PRESENT
play
run
ride

FUTURE
will play
will run
will ride

TITLE: _____

_____
_____
_____
_____
_____
_____

DAILY WRITING 3

Name _____ © GRØW Publications 89

Write a paragraph using this information.

| **The Earth** |
| - our planet |
| - round like a big ball |
| - spinning smoothly |
| - spins around once in 24 hours |

TITLE: _____

_____
_____
_____
_____
_____

DAILY WRITING 3

Name _____ © GRØW Publications 90

When you decide to start a new paragraph, you change
_____ , _____ , _____ or _____ .

Decide where you would start paragraphs in this story. Mark the place with a ¶ sign.

I have made a big decision. I'm going to give my little brother away. I know my mom might not like it, but it has to be done. Yesterday he snuck into my room when I was at school. He tore my room apart. I was so upset when I came home, I said, "Mom, how could you let him do this?" "Now, you know he's just a baby," she said.

Teacher Notes - DAILY WRITING - Grade 3

Answers/Comments — 88

Student stories will vary. Allow extra time for this exercise. Remind your students that the words in the boxes are <u>action</u> <u>verbs</u> or words that show action. They will be deciding if they want their story to happen in the past, present, or future. Be looking for a story that one of your students wrote in which they inappropriately changed tenses. You may want to model writing a story using the same verb tense.

Topics

Parts of Speech
Verb

Grammar/Usage
Verb Tense

Answers/Comments — 89

Student designed paragraphs will vary. Again today, allow extra time to complete this exercise. Review the term <u>paragraph</u> with your class. A paragraph contains several ideas about the same topic or the words of one speaker. The first line in a paragraph is indented, and a paragraph is shaped like a school bus. New paragraphs are formed when the idea, time, place or speaker change. Have your students try using paragraphing in their own stories.

Topics

Mechanics
Paragraphing
Paragraph structure

Answers/Comments — 90

Your students should put the paragraph sign before the word yesterday and before mom's words " Now you know." Take the time to discuss "why" the paragraphs changed. As part of editing, you can now expect your students to be checking for:

1. Does my story make sense?
2. Punctuation (. ! ? " " ,)
3. Spelling
4. Capitalization
5. Paragraphing

You may want to make an editing checklist for students to use with each story.

Topics

Writing Process
Proofreading/Editing
Standard Editing Notation

Mechanics
Paragraphing
Paragraph Structure, Dialogue

Permission granted to copy student pages for purchaser's class. <u>It is unlawful</u> to copy the teacher materials.
© GRØW Publications

DAILY WRITING 3

Name _____ © GRØW Publications   91

After reading the two titles below, write what you think each story is going to be about.

☐ MY DOG   ☐ BUTTERFLY DISCOVERY

_____   _____
_____   _____
_____   _____

Check the one you think you would rather read. Why did you choose it?

_____

DAILY WRITING 3

Name _____ © GRØW Publications   92

Decide what punctuation and capitalization choice is correct in each line below. Fill in the circle of the best choice.

(1) **Chickenpox is a virus. It mainly happens to <u>children When</u>**
(2) **someone has chickenpox, he or she is tired and has a <u>fever, It</u>**
(3) **also causes a red, itchy rash. <u>It's</u> not any fun to have chickenpox.**

1. ○ children when
   ○ children, When
   ○ children. When
   ○ Correct as is.

2. ○ fever, it
   ○ fever. It
   ○ fever it
   ○ Correct as is.

3. ○ it's
   ○ its
   ○ I'ts
   ○ Correct as is.

DAILY WRITING 3

Name _____   93

Write a story that is the opposite of this one, on the back of this strip or on another sheet of paper.

My Big Sis

My big sister is always nice to me. She gives me everything I want. If I ask her, "Can I have a piece of gum?"

She says, "Sure."

If I ask her to take me to the park, she says, "I'd love to." I'm really lucky to have such a great sister.

© GRØW Publications

Teacher Notes - DAILY WRITING - Grade 3

Answers/Comments — 91

Student work should reflect an understanding of the concepts involved in this activity.
Reinforce the importance of titles: they give the reader a hint of what a story is going to be about, and arouse the readers' curiosity. Ask your students to think about the titles of the stories they are working on and decide if a reader would choose to read their story because of its "catchy" title.

Topics
Author's Craft
Titles

Answers/Comments — 92

1. **children. When**
2. **fever. It**
3. **Correct as is**

This a format your students will need to become familiar with as they approach the time when they may be taking a standardized test. Discuss the format with them, especially noticing the relationship of the underlined words on the numbered lines to the numbers below.

Topics
Writing Process
Proofreading/Editing
Punctuation, Capitalization

Grammar/Usage
Contractions

Answers/Comments — 93

Student stories will vary.
It will be fun to see just how "opposite" your students' stories can be. Review the term <u>antonym</u> with your class. Two words that are the opposite of each other are antonyms. Often, writers will use opposites to build a contrast that emphasizes their meaning. The speed of a gazelle compared to that of a turtle would be an example of an opposite used to create a certain effect.

Topics
Grammar/Usage
Antonyms

Permission granted to copy student pages for purchaser's class. It is unlawful to copy the teacher materials.
© GRØW Publications

DAILY WRITING 3

Name _____ © GRØW Publications

94

Authors choose their words to build a picture in their readers' minds. Use the synonym groups to help you write a short story. Circle one word from each group to use in your story.

    find - locate - discover   want - desire - crave   key - answer - solution

_____
_____
_____
_____

_____

DAILY WRITING 3

Name _____

95

Make the sentences below sound more like the way we talk by crossing out incorrect words and putting the correct words above them.

Me and Pat don't like nothing better than a game of soccer. Me and him make the most goals. Me and the other students in our class play every recess. I won't never miss a soccer game.

© GRØW Publications

DAILY WRITING 3

Name _____ © GRØW Publications

96

An **apostrophe** (') is used to show possession.

   For example: **monkey's house** means **1 monkey owns 1 house**

If you move the **apostrophe**, the meaning changes.

   For example: **monkeys' house** means **two or more monkeys own 1 house**

Draw pictures to show what each of these possessives mean.

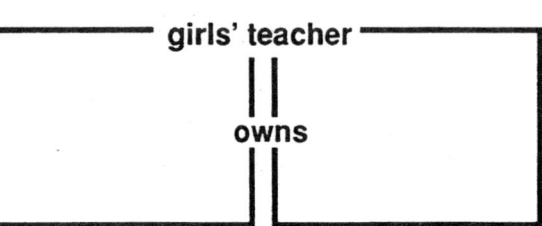
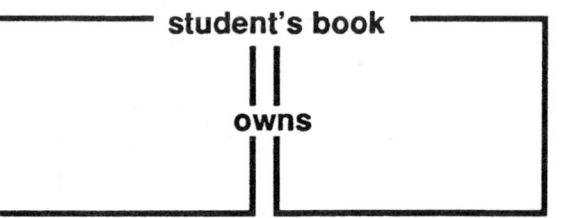

Teacher Notes - DAILY WRITING - Grade 3

Answers/Comments — 94

Student work will vary.
Student stories should have at least two to three sentences in them. This is a good time to introduce your students to a simple thesaurus. Compare the features in the thesaurus to those in the dictionary. Students who become good writers are able to use interesting words to help build pictures for their readers, and a thesaurus can provide assistance in this regard.

Topics
Grammar/Usage
Synonyms

Answers/Comments — 95

<u>Pat and I</u> don't like <u>anything</u> better than a game of soccer. <u>He and I</u> make the most goals. <u>We</u> and the other students in our class play every recess. I won't <u>ever</u> miss a soccer game or I <u>will never</u> miss a soccer game.

When words are combined to form sentences, there are rules of grammar that must be followed. The three rules highlighted in this activity are naming self last, avoiding the use of a double negative, and using the proper pronoun "we."

Topics
Grammar/Usage
Double Negatives, Naming Self Last

Parts of Speech
Pronoun

Answers/Comments — 96

Student drawings should show: 2 or more girls, one teacher; one student, one book. Extend this activity by asking your students to write and draw several examples on the backs of their activity strips. Your students should be able to use this strategy of visualizing their writing when they are editing their stories. To have students insert information automatically during the drafting stage is always a goal for which students should be striving. The less attention students need to pay to grammar and mechanics, the more they will be able to concentrate on the organization and craft of writing.

Topics
Parts of Speech
Noun
Possessive Noun

DAILY WRITING 3

Name _____ 97

If you were writing a news report about your school, what things could you write about? Make a list.

1. _____ 5. _____

2. _____ 6. _____

3. _____ 7. _____

4. _____ 8. _____

© GRØW Publications

DAILY WRITING 3

Name _____ © GRØW Publications 98

Choose one of the ideas from your list in Activity 97. Use the map below to help you think of important details that tell who, what, where, and when.

TOPIC

© GRØW Publications

DAILY WRITING 3

Name _____ © GRØW Publications 99

Use your map from Activity 98 to write a paragraph about your topic for the newspaper.

TOPIC SENTENCE ▷ _____

DETAILS ▷ _____

_____

_____

_____

_____

Teacher Notes - DAILY WRITING - Grade 3

Answers/Comments — 97

Student lists might include information about new school equipment, the teachers, principal, and other things taking place in your school. Writing about school events gives students an opportunity to do a different type of writing. Your students will be using their lists in Activity 98. If time permits, share an actual newspaper article with your students. Items from the newspaper almost always include the who, what, where, and when of the story.

Topics
Writing Process
Prewriting
Brainstorming, Form Selection

Answers/Comments — 98

Student maps will vary.
Your students will be using their maps to help them write a paragraph tomorrow. By now, they should understand the importance of retrieving what is known about a topic. This is important no matter what genre of writing is being utilized. Even fiction, to be believable, often uses real places, characters built on real people, and frequently includes incidents that have actually occurred.

Topics
Writing Process
Prewriting
Mapping/Clustering

Answers/Comments — 99

Individual topic sentences and accompanying details will vary. Introduce or review with your students the term <u>topic sentence</u>. The topic sentence tells what your paragraph is going to be about. Model a topic sentence on the board or overhead for your students. You may want to use one of these sentences:
* *At Morgan Elementary, students enjoy eating in the cafeteria.*
* *Recess at Morgan Elementary is sometimes different.*

After writing a topic sentence, your students can then use their maps to add details to their paragraphs.

Topics
Author's Craft
Organizational Pattern
Topic Sentence, Details

Permission granted to copy student pages for purchaser's class. It is unlawful to copy the teacher materials.
© GRØW Publications

DAILY WRITING 3

Name _____ © GROW Publications 100

Use these notes that Tavares took about koalas to write a paragraph.

KOALAS
- world's cutest animal
- thick, fuzzy fur
- marsupials (pouch for babies)
- not bears
- not related to bears

TOPIC SENTENCE _____
DETAILS _____
_____
_____
_____
_____

DAILY WRITING 3

Name _____ 101

The topic sentence is missing from the paragraph below. Mark the sentence that fits best by filling in the circle beside the one you chose.

_____
_____ . They graze like deer and hop like rabbits. Kangaroos also go without water like camels.

○ Kangaroos are very hard to describe.
○ Kangaroos run fast.
○ Kangaroos live in Australia.
○ Some kangaroos can go for weeks, even months, without water.

© GROW Publications

DAILY WRITING 3

Name _____ 102

Choose the answer that best develops the topic sentence that is given.

1. **We made pancakes for breakfast.**
   ○ My favorite food is waffles. It's my mom's favorite, too.
   ○ First we made the batter. Then we cooked them.
   ○ Sometimes we make french toast for lunch.
   ○ Breakfast is the best part of the day.

2. **There are many different kinds of dogs.**
   ○ I like poodles. My sister likes chows.
   ○ Our dog is a collie. He looks just like Lassie.
   ○ My mom let me have a dog. I have to feed and water her.
   ○ Some dogs are small, and others are large. There are ones with short fur and some with long fur.

© GROW Publications

Teacher Notes - DAILY WRITING - Grade 3

Answers/Comments　　　　　　　　　　　　　　　　　　　　　100

Student work will vary. As students continue to progress through school, this format, especially in the areas of non-fiction writing, will become more and more important. Simplistic tasks for getting your students to use the structure of a paragraph may include writing:
1. Animal reports
2. News reports
3. Biographies
4. Reports targeting social studies and science topics

Topics
Author's Craft
Organizational Pattern
Topic Sentence, Details

Answers/Comments　　　　　　　　　　　　　　　　　　　　　101

Kangaroos are very hard to describe.
If you have students who finish early, you may want to put this paragraph on the board for students to find the topic sentence..

Soccer balls, baseballs and basketballs are round. Footballs are shaped like an oval.
* Sports are fun to play.　　　　　　* I play different sports.
* Balls come in different shapes.　　* Have you ever wanted to play soccer?

Answer: Balls come in different shapes.

Topics
Author's Craft
Organizational Pattern
Topic Sentence, Details

Answers/Comments　　　　　　　　　　　　　　　　　　　　　102

1. First we made the batter. Then we cooked them.
2. Some dogs are small, and others are large. There are ones with short fur and some with long fur.
The format used in this warm-up will also be found on standardized tests. Extend the activity by asking your students, in pairs if possible, to choose a topic. Instruct them to write the topic sentence and details just like in the activity. Allow time for them to exchange their paragraphs.

Topics
Author's Craft
Organizational Pattern
Topic Sentence, Details

Permission granted to copy student pages for purchaser's class. It is unlawful to copy the teacher materials.
© GRØW Publications

Daily Writing 3

Name ____ © GRØW Publications   103

Find the word that best completes each sentence. Mark your answer.

1. The box felt much ____ than she thought it would be.
   - ○ heavy
   - ○ heavily
   - ○ heaviest
   - ○ heavier

2. ____ house burned to the ground.
   - ○ Their
   - ○ They
   - ○ These
   - ○ They're

3. The ____ voices came from the library.
   - ○ girl
   - ○ girl's
   - ○ girls
   - ○ girls's

4. That ____ toys are all broken.
   - ○ boy's
   - ○ boys's
   - ○ boys
   - ○ boys'

Daily Writing 3

Name ____ © GRØW Publications   104

For each number, mark the sentence that is complete and is written correctly.

- ○ He saw the man who.
- ○ Big and furry.
- ○ Making my bed.
- ○ The boy sat on the stairs.

- ○ Dog helping us.
- ○ Coming to the door.
- ○ The dog is at our house.
- ○ In the kitchen.

- ○ When we sit in the bus.
- ○ The boys play football.
- ○ The cat walk on the fence.
- ○ The horse jump high.

- ○ Grandpa talked to me and she?
- ○ Did you ask he?
- ○ Can you come to my party?
- ○ How many of they are there?

Daily Writing 3

Name ____ © GRØW Publications   105

Read each sentence and decide which part, if any, needs a capital letter. If no capital letters are missing, fill in the circle that goes with the word "None." Mark your answer by filling in the circle.

1. Mary and | i read | the book. | None
2. we need | those papers | finished. | None
3. Her party | will be | next wednesday. | None
4. His Aunt | sue lives | in Colorado. | None
5. My sister | started her letter | "dear Julie.". | None

Teacher Notes - DAILY WRITING - Grade 3

Answers/Comments — 103

1. heavier   2. Their   3. girl's   4. boy's

This exercise (and Activity 101) have been written with the language expression portion of a standardized test in mind. Students need to be aware of content as well as feel comfortable with the format of the test if they are to do their best. This lesson covers superlatives and possessives. Your students may want to write some of their own examples of test questions to share with each other.

Topics
Parts of Speech
Noun
Possessive Noun

Answers/Comments — 104

The boy sat...; The dog...; The boys...; Can you...

This exercise covers complete and incomplete sentences. It also requires the students to use proper grammar. It will be important for them to read each sentence carefully and to ask themselves questions such as the following:
1. Is it a complete thought or idea?
2. Does it sound like the way we should talk?

If they can answer yes to both of these questions, that sentence will be the correct answer.

Topics
Sentences
Structure
Complete Sentences, Sentence Fragments

Answers/Comments — 105

1. Mary and <u>I</u>   2. <u>W</u>e need   3. next <u>W</u>ednesday   4. <u>S</u>ue lives
5. "<u>D</u>ear Julie."

This is probably one of the most confusing formats on the standardized tests for students. First, it is important for them to understand that these are sentences. The slashes between groups of words were put in randomly. Sometimes there may be two words and sometimes there may be three words. You might choose to have your class write a sentence like the ones in this activity to exchange with classmates.

Topics
Writing Process
Proofreading/Editing
Capitalization

Permission granted to copy student pages for purchaser's class. It is unlawful to copy the teacher materials.
© GRØW Publications

Daily Writing 3

Name _____

For each number, find the sentence that is written correctly and has the correct capitalization and punctuation.

1.
- ○ We went to Orlando, Florida on Monday.
- ○ My sister lives in dallas, Texas.
- ○ The letter was sent to Denver, colorado by mistake.
- ○ Chicago Illinois is a very large city.

2.
- ○ Turquoise lake is beautiful.
- ○ President Lincoln was shot in Ford's Theater.
- ○ We will be visiting Disney world this summer.
- ○ We live in the rocky mountains.

© GRØW Publications

Daily Writing 3

Name _____

Match the term with its meaning.

- BRAINSTORMING ●   ● Thinking of ideas to put into a story.
- DRAFTING ●   ● Checking capitals, punctuation, spelling, and paragraphing.
- REVISING ●   ● Writing a story down.
- EDITING/PROOFREADING ●   ● Preparing a piece of writing for others to read.
- PUBLISHING ●   ● Changing the <u>ideas</u> in a story so they sound better or clearer.

© GRØW Publications

Daily Writing 3

Name _____   © GRØW Publications

Use the kinds of writing listed in the box to answer the following questions.

Fiction	Report Writing
Poetry	Letters
News Reporting	
Plays	Sports Events
Personal Narrative	
Others	

What kind of writing do you do the most? _____

What kind of writing is easy for you? _____

What kind of writing would be a challenge for you? _____

Why would it be a challenge?

_____

_____

Teacher Notes - DAILY WRITING - Grade 3

Answers/Comments — 106

1. We went to Orlando, Florida on Monday. 2. President Lincoln was shot in Ford's Theater.

Your students will need to know how to capitalize and punctuate dates, cities and states, the greeting and closing of a letter, and proper nouns such as Turquoise Lake, Ford's Theater, etc. Continually reinforce the reasons for capitalizing words (I, days of the week, months of the year, people's names, particular places, months, cities and states, book titles, etc.).

Topics
Mechanics
Capitalization
Proper Noun

Answers/Comments — 107

Editing/Proofreading---checking capitals, punctuation, spelling and paragraphing. *Revising*---Changing the <u>ideas</u> in a story so they sound better or are clearer. *Publishing*---Preparing a piece of writing for others to read. *Brainstorming*---Thinking of ideas to put into a story. *Drafting*---Writing a story down in its first forms.

This particular warm-up activity checks your students' understandings of some of the different terms associated with the writing process.

Topics
Student/Teacher Assessment
Student and Teacher Assessment

Answers/Comments — 108

Student answers will vary. This list is representative of the kinds of writing in which students may be engaged. Many other writing needs could be added such as writing in math, songs, instructions on how to do something, etc. If your students are continually choosing to write the same thing, you have the opportunity to move them in a new direction towards a new challenge.

Topics
Writing Process   **Student/Teacher Assessment**
Prewriting, Drafting   Student and Teacher Assessment
Form Selection

Permission granted to copy student pages for purchaser's class. It is unlawful to copy the teacher materials.
© GROW Publications

DAILY WRITING 3

109

Make a list of **where** you get ideas for things to write about.

1. _____
2. _____
3. _____
4. _____
5. _____
6. _____
7. _____
8. _____

© GRØW Publications

DAILY WRITING 3

Name _____ © GRØW Publications

110

A piece of writing that is **focused** clearly stays on the same topic. Read this paragraph, then answer the questions.

    I am the luckiest kid in the school to have Mrs. Blakemore for a teacher. She treats all of us like we're really special. In the morning, she greets each of us with a big smile and a warm hello. We play games on Fridays and have pizza parties.

Does this story stay **focused**? _____

What makes you say that? _____

© GRØW Publications

DAILY WRITING 3

Name _____

111

1. Match the revision marks with when you would use them.

    CROSSING OUT ●   ● Adding a word or a phrase.

    CARET ^ ●   ● Moving words or ideas.

    SYMBOLS * ♥ ♦ etc. ●   ● Adding long sentences or paragraphs.

    The boy went... ●   ● Taking out words or ideas that are not needed.

2. "Revision" means _____

© GRØW Publications

Teacher Notes - DAILY WRITING - Grade 3

Answers/Comments   109

Some possible student answers may include: from watching people, books I read, things I'm interested in learning more about, etc.
When students say, "I don't have anything to write about," it is often assumed that they just aren't thinking. It is easy for some students to come up with many different topics to research or write about. After your students have completed this activity, facilitate a class sharing time. Ask students to identify some of the places where they get ideas for topics. Record student responses on a chart paper that can be left up in the classroom for future reference.

Topics   **Writing Process**
Prewriting
Topic Selection

Answers/Comments   110

Does the story stay focused? (No, the story did not stay focused.) What makes you say that? (The first part was about the teacher. The last part was about activities that are done in Mrs. Blakemore's classroom.) If additional writing space is needed, instruct the class to finish writing the answer to the second question on the backs of their activity strips or other sheets of paper. Ask your students to read their pieces of writing and decide if their stories stayed focused on their topics.

Topics   **Student/Teacher Assessment**
Student and Teacher Assessment

Answers/Comments   111

Crossing out---taking out words or ideas that are not needed.
Carets (^)---adding a word or phrase. *Symbols*---adding long sentences or paragraphs. *Circling and arrows* ---moving words or ideas. Revision is "seeing" your story again with a reader in mind and making changes that will make the story sound better or make the ideas clearer.
Underscore the importance of revision and being a good writer.

Topics   **Writing Process**   **Student/Teacher Assessment**
Revising   Student and Teacher Assessment
Revision Strategies

Permission granted to copy student pages for purchaser's class. It is unlawful to copy the teacher materials.
© GRØW Publications

DAILY WRITING 3

Name _____

112

One of the sentences in the paragraph is called a **run-on** sentence. Can you fix it?

Did you know there are bears in Yellowstone Park? Well, let me tell you about the one that ate our picnic lunch. We found a beautiful spot under the trees to spread out our picnic lunch then we went to the river to play and then we heard noises coming from where we had left our lunch and then we ran back to see what was going on. To our surprise, a bear was sitting in the middle of our picnic spot enjoying the last of our food.

© GRØW Publications

DAILY WRITING 3

Name _____

113

Think of a place you enjoy going. Describe it using each of the senses listed below.

SEE	HEAR	FEEL

SMELL	TASTE	Name the place.

© GRØW Publications

DAILY WRITING 3

Name _____ © GRØW Publications

114

Use your information from Activity 113 to write a descriptive paragraph about your favorite place.

_____
_____
_____
_____

Teacher Notes - DAILY WRITING - Grade 3

Answers/Comments　　　　　　　　　　　　　　　　　　　　　　112

Sentence three is a run-on. This sentence should be broken into smaller ones that contain less information.
Start this exercise by having the class predict what a run-on sentence might look like. Run-on sentences are two (or more) separate thoughts that run together without the appropriate punctuation marks. Then, have students complete the activity strip looking for the run-on sentence and correcting it. Students should be using ending punctuation marks during the drafting stage of their writing.

Topics
Sentences
Structure
Run-on Sentences

Answers/Comments　　　　　　　　　　　　　　　　　　　　　　113

Student answers will vary. Smell and taste may be hard for your students to describe, especially depending on the place students indicate they like visit. Students do not need to fill in a category if it does not fit with their place. Encourage the class to use their senses in the stories they are writing today. Also, be sure your students make the reading/writing connection by searching for descriptive passages while reading. Your students will need the information from this exercise to complete Activity 114.

Topics
Author's Craft
Descriptive Language

Answers/Comments　　　　　　　　　　　　　　　　　　　　　　114

Paragraphs will vary. Remind your students to start their paragraphs with leads that will "hook" their readers. Conclude by having your class share their paragraphs in a small group. Each student could use their paragraph as a setting for a fiction story or a personal narrative. In both of these types of stories it is important to establish the place (setting) of the story.

Topics
Author's Craft
Descriptive Language

Permission granted to copy student pages for purchaser's class. It is unlawful to copy the teacher materials.
© GRØW Publications

DAILY WRITING 3

Name _____ © GROW Publications 115

Select one of the problems listed below or write one of your own. Then complete the map with your plan to write a fiction story.

	CHARACTERS	SETTING
Your bike is missing.	PROBLEM	SOLUTION
The lights go off and its pitch dark.		
You find a creature from outer space.		

✂ (Your own) _____

DAILY WRITING 3

Name _____ © GROW Publications 116

Use your plan from Activity 115 to complete the character sketch below.

MAIN CHARACTER: _____

Looks like	**Acts like**	**Says**

DAILY WRITING 3

Name _____ 117

Using comparisons in a story helps give the reader a better picture of what you're trying to describe. Add comparisons to this story.

What a great day for fishing. The water was <u>as smooth as</u> _____. I threw my line in and watched the hook sink to the bottom. Suddenly, a fish pounced on the hook. It swam away <u>as fast as</u> _____. I jerked my pole back. Up came my hook <u>as empty as</u> _____.

© GROW Publications

Teacher Notes - DAILY WRITING - Grade 3

Answers/Comments `115`

Students' completed maps will vary. Fiction stories can be a difficult kind of writing for some students. A good fiction story often has the plot structure outlined in this activity. Thinking through all of the elements of a fiction story involves a great deal of planning. Fiction stories that students write without going through the planning stage are often unfocused, sometimes missing well thought out characters or a proper structure. Your students will use their plans in Activity 116.

Topics
Author's Craft
Organizational Pattern
Problem, Events, Solution

Answers/Comments `116`

Student character sketches will vary.
Developing a character to put in a story is an important part of making a character believable. If you study Marc Brown's books about Arthur, you begin to know how a character will act and what he or she will say no matter which selection of his you are reading. Even if a student is writing about his or her little sister, the character should be developed well enough for the reader to say, "I really know what your little sister is like."

Topics
Author's Craft
Develops Story Characters

Answers/Comments `117`

Students' choice of comparisons will vary.
Comparisons are fun for writers to use and readers to read. If any of your students begin to use them in the stories they write, they will find that the other students respond to their stories with a great deal of enthusiasm. Remind the class that frequently poets and authors use similes and metaphors to surprise the reader, and to help describe something in a more vivid, interesting way.

Topics
Author's Craft
Figurative Language

Permission granted to copy student pages for purchaser's class. It is unlawful to copy the teacher materials.
© GRØW Publications

DAILY WRITING 3

Name _____ © GRØW Publications

118

A simple sentence has two parts, the **subject** and the **predicate**.

SUBJECT: tells who or what the sentence is about.

PREDICATE: tells what the subject is or does.

In this example, the subject is underlined once, the predicate twice.

<u>Trees</u> <u><u>give us many different things.</u></u>

Write three more simple sentences. Underline each subject once and each predicate twice.

1. _____
2. _____
3. _____

DAILY WRITING 3

Name _____ © GRØW Publications

119

Complete the timeline with information from each period of <u>your</u> life.

- Birth →
- Age 1-2 →
- Age 3-4 →
- Kindergarten →
- Grade 1 →
- Grade 2 →
- Grade 3 →

DAILY WRITING 3

Name _____

120

Revise this story so that it makes more sense.

When I was five years old, I started kindergarten. I was so scared I cried for the first week. Preschool was so much fun. I loved painting. I must have taken home five pictures every time I went. When I was a baby, I was bald, I mean, light bulb bald. Now I'm in third grade. It's my favorite because I really like my teacher.

© GRØW Publications

Teacher Notes - DAILY WRITING - Grade 3

Answers/Comments [118]

Student sentences should include a subject and predicate underlined correctly.
Sentence fragments are missing the subject or the predicate. You may want your class to have an opportunity to use the terms subject and predicate by giving them sentence fragments and asking what is missing. Here are some examples that you can use:
* A big car
* crashed on the bridge
* Children from our school
* dipped the brush in the paint
* built a new road
* Soon the door

Topics

Sentences
Parts
Subject, Predicate

Sentences
Structure
Simple Sentences

Answers/Comments [119]

Completed timelines will vary.
A timeline is a good way for students to explore new topics to write about. It is also a way to explore the structure of biographies. Researching famous people, such as presidents and other leaders, may be of interest to some of your students. They need to be aware that, typically, biographies are written in chronological order.

Topics

Writing Process
Drafting
Organized Structure

Writing Process
Prewriting
Topic Selection

Answers/Comments [120]

Rearrange the sentences in the paragraph: When I was a baby... Preschool... I loved... I must have... When I was five... Now I'm...
This activity reinforces sequence and chronological order. Be sure to promote the reading/writing connection by sharing a biography with your students. At this point, you may want to review some of the organizational structures your students will find in reading, and be able to utilize in writing.

Topics

Writing Process
Revising
Story Makes Sense

Permission granted to copy student pages for purchaser's class. It is unlawful to copy the teacher materials.
© GRØW Publications

DAILY WRITING 3

Name _____ © GROW Publications 121

Write a conversation between you and your teacher. Be sure to write down who is speaking and use punctuation marks correctly.

_____
_____
_____
_____
_____
_____
_____
_____
_____

DAILY WRITING 3

Name _____ © GROW Publications 122

Match the ending mark with when you use it.

PERIOD ●   ● to show strong feeling
QUESTION MARK ●   ● to tell something or order someone to do something
EXCLAMATION MARK ● ● to ask a question

Write a sentence that shows strong feeling for each of the emotions listed below.

SURPRISE _____

ANGER _____

HAPPINESS _____

DAILY WRITING 3

Name _____ © GROW Publications 123

Write a sentence that shows strong feeling.

_____

Write a sentence that asks a question.

_____

Write a sentence that tells something.

_____

Write a sentence that tells someone to do something.

_____

Teacher Notes - DAILY WRITING - Grade 3

Answers/Comments   121

Student writing will vary.
Your class may enjoy working in pairs on this activity. If they have difficulty remembering how to punctuate their sentences, place the two examples below on the board for them to use as a model:
* My teacher said, "You really work hard."
* "You really work hard," my teacher said.

Review the importance of using conversation in your students' writing each day.

Topics

Author's Craft
Dialogue

Mechanics
Capitalization
Direct Quote

Answers/Comments   122

Period---to tell something or order someone to do something. *Question mark*---to ask a quesytion. *Exclamation mark*---to show strong feeling. **The three sentences your students write should all end with an exclamation mark.**

Stress with your students the importance of ending punctuation marks. They help the reader get a clearer idea of the author's message, by communicating an emotion such as excitement, or a stong feeling.

Topics

Mechanics
Punctuation
End of Sentence (. ! ?)

Answers/Comments   123

Student sentences should demonstrate an understanding of the required task.

The four types of sentences your students are writing in this activity are: exclamatory, interrogative, declarative, and imperative. You should decide whether the more technical terms are important for your students to know and understand. It is important for them to realize that every sentence written or read fits into one of these four categories.

Topics

Sentences
Types
Declarative, Interrogative, Exclamatory, Imperative

Permission granted to copy student pages for purchaser's class. It is unlawful to copy the teacher materials.
© GRØW Publications

DAILY WRITING 3

Name _____ 124

TOPIC: _____

Choose a topic that you could write about. These words might help you.

Make a list of everything you would include in your story.

| person |
| place |
| thing |

_____
_____
_____
_____
_____
_____

© GRØW Publications

DAILY WRITING 3

Name _____ 125

Use your topic and list from Activity 124 to write 2 good **leads** for your story.

Remember: **leads** are supposed to make the reader want to read on. Leads may start with **conversation, action, thinking in your head, a description, etc.**

LEAD 1 _____
_____

LEAD 2 _____
_____

© GRØW Publications

DAILY WRITING 3

Name _____ © GRØW Publications 126

Creative endings take the surprise. They fit with the story and yet they aren't endings like these: →

"They lived happily ever after."
"He woke up. It was just a dream."
"She never went there again."

Write a brief creative ending that surprised you from a story you read or have written.

_____
_____
_____

Teacher Notes - DAILY WRITING - Grade 3

Answers/Comments [124]

Students' topics and details will vary.
Students will be using their topics and brainstormed lists in Activity 125. Your class, through previous instruction, should be comfortable starting their stories in this way. By generating ideas targeting what they know about a topic, writers are able to use important details in their stories.

Topics
Writing Process
Prewriting
Brainstorming

Writing Process
Drafting
Topics Developed with Details

Answers/Comments [125]

Students' leads will vary.
This time of year is fun in third grade because many of your students are realizing that they are very good writers. Be sure to encourage students who are trying to come up with good leads as well as celebrating when a student has managed to really "hook" his or her readers. Continue to have your class notice leads in the books, poems, and articles they are completing. Reading takes on new meaning when students begin to read like writers.

Topics
Author's Craft
Creative Leads

Answers/Comments [126]

The endings students have chosen will vary.
Students In third grade seem to work very hard on becoming fluent writers, using proper punctuation, capitalization, and spelling. They also grow in the craft of writing often using good leads, conversation, and descriptive language. Endings seem to be one of the most difficult parts of a story for third graders to compose. It is helpful for classmates to be able to confer with each other about story endings.

Topics
Author's Craft
Creative Endings

Permission granted to copy student pages for purchaser's class. It is unlawful to copy the teacher materials.
© GRØW Publications

DAILY WRITING 3

Name _____ 127

Change the verbs in this story to **strong verbs** so the reader has a better picture of what is happening.

    Our class was playing tag at school yesterday. I was it. I <u>went</u> after Joe and
                                                                                                           (1)
<u>got</u> him. He turned around to tag me back but I <u>moved</u> away. So he took off after Jill.
(2)   (3)
She <u>went</u> to hide behind Jerome. Jerome <u>saw</u> what she was going to do and tricked
    (4)   (5)
her by <u>moving</u> to the side. Joe <u>ran</u> after Jill and caught her by the tail of her shirt.
      (6)   (7)
Today, when we go out to recess, Jill will be "it."

© GRØW Publications

DAILY WRITING 3

Name _____ 128

Write the titles of 3 books or movies you know.

1. _____

2. _____

3. _____

Circle the title that you like the best and tell why you like it.

_____

_____

© GRØW Publications

DAILY WRITING 3

Name _____ 129

Make a list of all of the kinds of words that need to be capitalized.

_____ _____

_____ _____

_____ _____

_____ _____

© GRØW Publications

Teacher Notes - *DAILY WRITING* - Grade 3

Answers/Comments   127

Words your students may think of using could include:
1. went - charged, tore, flew, zoomed
2. got - captured, caught
3. moved - dodged, jerked
4. went - moved, ran
5. saw - spotted, spied
6. moving - turning, slipping
7. ran - zipped, tore, scurried.

Allow time for students to share their revised paragraphs with partners or in small groups.

Topics
Author's Craft
Strong Verbs

Answers/Comments   128

Specific titles and corresponding reasons will vary.
For this warm-up activity, students can use any books or movies they can think of. Consider having a variety of books from the library for students to examine. To further explore the topic of titles, divide your students into small groups. Ask each group to discuss what makes a good title, making a list of their answers on chart paper to share with the rest of the class.

Topics
Author's Craft
Titles

Answers/Comments   129

Your students' lists may include: days of the week, months of the year, cities, states, counties, peoples' names, bodies of water, planets, titles of books.

Remind your students that words naming a particular person, place or thing are called proper nouns.

Topics
Parts of Speech
Noun
Proper Noun

Permission granted to copy student pages for purchaser's class. It is unlawful to copy the teacher materials.
© GRØW Publications

DAILY WRITING 3

Name _____ © GRØW Publications 130

New paragraphs start when the **time**, **place**, **idea**, and/or **speaker** changes. Place a ¶ sign where new paragraphs should be started in this story.

<u>The Platypus</u>

Of all the animals on earth, the only ones that lay eggs are the duck-billed platypus and the spiny anteater. They are called monotremes. When the platypus was first discovered, scientists were really confused. This animal had webbed feet like a duck and a flat tail like a beaver, Its fur is thick like a mammal and it lays eggs like a reptile. The platypus has an enormous appetite. It weighs about 4 pounds and can eat up to 2 pounds of food a day.

DAILY WRITING 3

Name _____ © GRØW Publications 131

Study these examples of how to punctuate sentences when people are speaking.

    "Can I go to the movies tonight?" I asked.

    My mom said, "Not until your room is cleaned."

    "That would take all night! I think I'll watch a movie on TV," I said.

Write a brief conversation between you and your mom, or someone else in your family.

_____

_____

_____

DAILY WRITING 3

Name _____ 132

Write a short letter on another sheet of paper. Use this checklist <u>after</u> you have written the letter. Put a smile on the face for each one that checks out OK.

1. **Date on the right hand side.**

2. **Date is correctly written.**
   (May 5, 1997)

3. **Greeting is capitalized, and followed by a comma.**  (Dear Jerome,)

4. **First paragraph is indented.**

5. **Closing has the first word capitalized.** (Your friend,)

6. **I signed my name below the closing.**

© GRØW Publications

Teacher Notes - DAILY WRITING - Grade 3

Answers/Comments — 130

New Paragraph -- Of all the...
New Paragraph -- When the platypus was first ...
New Paragraph -- The platypus has an ...

Discuss the reasons why the paragraphs need to be indented. Many paragraphs such as the second one changed both time and idea. This is not unusual occurrence when examining why a new paragraph was formed.

Topics

Writing Process	Mechanics
Proofreading/Editing	Paragraphing
Standard Editing Notation	Indenting

Answers/Comments — 131

Students' conversations will vary.
If your students run out of space while writing their conversations, ask them to finish their work on the backs of their activity strips. You may want to mention that a (!) or (?) is used as a sentence ending before the speaker's name but not before a period. Instead, a comma is placed before the word "said." Conversation is one of the ways authors show what a character is like and what is happening in a story.

Topics

Author's Craft	Mechanics
Dialogue	Capitalization
	Direct Quote

Answers/Comments — 132

Student letters will vary.
Begin this exercise by instructing each student to write a short letter on another piece of paper to someone he or she knows. After students complete their letters, they can use the checklist on the activity strip to see if they know all the parts of a letter. If a student has completed an item correctly, he or she may fill in the smiley face beside that item.

Topics

Mechanics
Capitalization
Greeting and Closing of a Letter

Permission granted to copy student pages for purchaser's class. It is unlawful to copy the teacher materials.
© GRØW Publications

Daily Writing 3

Name _____ © GROW Publications 133

The capitals and punctuation marks have been left out of these sentences. Fix them so they are okay.

<u>home run king</u>

henry (hank) aaron hit his 715th home run on april 8, 1974 he had been playing in the major leagues for 20 years his 715th homer broke babe ruths record now hank was the home run king of baseball what a day it was for him

Daily Writing 3

Name _____ © GROW Publications 134

Many things in this story are not said correctly. Fix them.

<u>Me and My Brother</u>

Me and my brother are not exactly best friends. He think I'm just a little kid. I can't understand why he don't let me go places with him. I'm always nice to his friends. In fact, I don't never let them out of my sight. I sticks to them like glue. Oh, here they comes now. I has to go. Bye!

Daily Writing 3

Name _____ 135

Read this paragraph. On the lines, list what the author did to make this paragraph interesting.

<u>The Clock Says "Go!"</u>

I glanced up at the clock. It was just three minutes until recess. I finished my last math problem and waited for the clock to say "Go!" On our way out the door, my friend grabbed her new soccer ball. It was another big game. We tore down to the big, grassy field and the game began.

Teacher Notes - DAILY WRITING - Grade 3

Answers/Comments　　133

<u>H</u>ome <u>R</u>un <u>K</u>ing (title)　<u>H</u>enry (<u>H</u>ank) <u>A</u>aron hit his 715th home run on <u>A</u>pril 8, 1974<u>.</u> <u>H</u>e had been playing in the major leagues for 20 years<u>.</u> <u>H</u>is 715th homer broke <u>B</u>abe <u>R</u>uth's record<u>.</u> <u>N</u>ow Hank was the home run king of baseball<u>.</u> <u>W</u>hat a day it was for him<u>!</u>

This may be a prime opportunity to ask your students how they know when to put in periods and capitals.

Topics

Mechanics
Capitalization
Beginning of Sentence

Mechanics
Punctuation
End of Sentence (. ! ?)

Answers/Comments　　134

<u>My Brother and I</u>
<u>My brother and I</u> are not exactly best friends. He <u>thinks</u> I'm just a little kid. I can't understand why he <u>doesn't</u> let me go places with him. I'm always nice to his friends. In fact, I don't <u>ever</u> let them out of my sight. I <u>stick</u> to them like glue. Oh, here they <u>come</u> now. I <u>have</u> to go. Bye!

Decide what other points you want to touch upon based on what you have seen in your students' writing. You will find examples of double negatives and verb tense in the story.

Topics

Writing Process
Proofreading/Editing
Standard Grammar

Answers/Comments　　135

Student responses may include some of these reasons:
1. a lead that "hooks" the reader
2. strong verbs
3. use of the senses
4. descriptive language
5. creative title and ending.

This is a good time to review the qualities of good writing. Reinforce with students the importance of spending more time to carefully craft their writing skills.

Topics

Author's Craft
Creative Endings, Titles

Permission granted to copy student pages for purchaser's class. <u>It is unlawful</u> to copy the teacher materials.
© GROW Publications

DAILY WRITING 3

136

Cross out words and add words using carets (^) so this paragraph makes more sense.

My mom took a new barbershop to get my hair cut. I was a new nervous wreck. What if he cut too short? What if I was bald when if I got out of that chair? How could she my mom do this to me?

What did you just do (circle one)?   Edit   Draft   Publish   Revise

---

DAILY WRITING 3

137

The author reread this paragraph and discovered that two sentences were missing. Use symbols to add the sentences where they belong in the paragaph.

On July 20, 1969, the first man stepped foot on the moon. A Russian space flight in 1964 sent the first woman into space. Many more flights were made. You may be interested in studying about space exploration.

☐ He was an American named Neil Armstrong.

☐ Valentina Terreshkova was the first woman cosmonaut.

DAILY WRITING 3

138

Adjectives are used to describe nouns. Think of two adjectives that could describe each of the nouns listed below.

_____ _____ school _____ _____ tree

_____ _____ water _____ _____ desk

_____ _____ pizza

_____ _____ baby

Teacher Notes - DAILY WRITING - Grade 3

Answers/Comments [136]

My mom took me to a new barbershop to get my hair cut. I was a ~~new~~ nervous wreck. What if he cuts it too short? What if I was bald when ~~if~~ I got out of that chair? How could ~~she~~ my mom do this to me? (or) How could she ~~my mom~~ do this to me?
What did you just do? **Revise**
Inform your class that carefully revising their writing usually will catch at least one mistake, and often many more. It is a crucial part of making sure you communicate clearly with an audience.

Topics
Writing Process
Revising
Story Makes Sense, Revision Strategies

Answers/Comments [137]

The first new sentence should go after the word "moon." The second new sentence should follow the words "first woman in space."
For this warm-up lesson your students may choose to use any symbol they want to. Common symbols include asterisks, stars, etc. The understanding you want your students to have is that just because there is no space left on the paper does not mean they can't fix things or add vital or interesting pieces of information.

Topics
Writing Process
Revising
Story makes sense, Revision strategies

Answers/Comments [138]

Student choice of adjectives will vary.
Continue this activity into your students' writing by asking them to refer to one of the stories they have written previously. Using the revision techniques they are familiar with, direct them to add adjectives to their own stories. Deliberately revising using adjectives is an excellent way to add description to a story.

Topics
Parts of Speech
Adjective

Permission granted to copy student pages for purchaser's class. It is unlawful to copy the teacher materials.
© GROW Publications

DAILY WRITING 3

Name _____ © GRØW Publications

139

Each of these words has two meanings. Write the two meanings in the boxes. Choose another word with two meanings. Write the word and its two meanings.

gum
- [ ]
- [ ]

fly
- [ ]
- [ ]

_____
- [ ]
- [ ]

DAILY WRITING 3

Name _____

140

Write a math story problem that would explain this concept. $1 + 2 = 2 + 1$

_____
_____
_____
_____
_____

© GRØW Publications

DAILY WRITING 3

Name _____

141

Think about your third grade year. Write or draw what you remember about the beginning, middle, and end of the year.

BEGINNING	MIDDLE	END

© GRØW Publications

Teacher Notes - DAILY WRITING - Grade 3

Answers/Comments | 139

gum-a sticky substance from certain trees, tissue around teeth.
fly-insect, move through the air with wings. Student sentences will vary.
These words are called homographs. They look the same but mean different things. It is important to be sure the meaning is clear when using a homograph in writing.

Topics
Grammar/Usage
Homophones/Homographs

Answers/Comments | 140

Story problems will vary, but might include something like this:
Shanae has one pencil in her hand and two in her desk. Gerome has two pencils in his hand and one in his desk. Both Shanae and Gerome have three pencils.

Writing across the curriculum moves writing from being a separate subject to becoming a tool for learning. Writing about a subject helps clarify and organize concepts and ideas. Since writing is thinking on paper, it helps you to assess your students' thought processes when you ask them to write down what they know about a topic.

Topics
Writing Process
Prewriting
Form Selection

Answers/Comments | 141

Students' writings or drawings will vary.
Expand this exercise by asking your third graders to write letters to next year's third graders. They can tell them about third grade including high points and challenges. Be sure to ask them to use the structure of beginning, middle, and end.

Topics
Author's Craft
Organizational Pattern
Beginning, Middle, End

Permission granted to copy student pages for purchaser's class. It is unlawful to copy the teacher materials.
© GRØW Publications

DAILY WRITING 3

Name _____ 142

Rate yourself on each of the areas.

	I'm really good.	I'm OK.	Still hard for me.
CHOOSING A TOPIC	1	2	3
DRAFTING MY STORY	1	2	3
REVISING MY STORY	1	2	3
EDITING MY STORY	1	2	3
WRITING LIKE AN AUTHOR	1	2	3

© GRØW Publications

DAILY WRITING 3

Name _____ 143

Connect each part of speech with its definition.

NOUN ●   ● describes a noun

ACTION VERB ●   ● shows possession

POSSESSIVE NOUN ●   ● names a person, place, or thing

ADJECTIVE ●   ● names a particular person, place, or thing

PROPER NOUN ●   ● shows action

© GRØW Publications

DAILY WRITING 3

Name _____ © GRØW Publications 144

Write a paragraph describing yourself as a writer to your fourth grade teacher. What are you good at? What are you still working on?

_____

_____

_____

_____

Teacher Notes - DAILY WRITING - Grade 3

Answers/Comments　　　142

Student ratings will vary.
To further explore your students' understanding of the writing process, ask them to jot down a few words that would explain each item listed. You may want the class to do this on the reverse sides of their activity strips or separate pieces of paper.

Topics　Student/Teacher Assessment
Student and Teacher Assessment

Answers/Comments　　　143

***Noun*---names a person, place or thing. *Action verb*---shows action. *Possessive noun*---shows possession. *Adjective*---describes a noun. *Proper noun*---names a particular peron, place or thing.** Allow your students to use a dictionary if they can't remember these terms. The point of this activity is for your students to remember that the words in the English language are classified into groups. This helps students acquire an understanding of language as well as supply a foundation for learning a different language.

Topics　Student/Teacher Assessment
Student and Teacher Assessment

Answers/Comments　　　144

Student letters will vary. Consider sending these letters on to next year's teacher(s) with a beginning and ending writing sample attached. It is interesting to see which students really have an idea of their strengths and needs as writers. When students grow in this area, they are able to build upon their strengths and target areas for growth.

Topics　Student/Teacher Assessment
Student and Teacher Assessment

Permission granted to copy student pages for purchaser's class. It is unlawful to copy the teacher materials.
© GRØW Publications

Four Easy Ways to Order — Order Today!

 Mail ETA
620 Lakeview Parkway
Vernon Hills, IL 60061-1838

Phone 800-445-5985
Fax 800-ETA-9326
E-mail info@etauniverse.com

Date	Purchase Order#	ETA Account	Tax Exempt #

Ship to: (Be sure to give street address—UPS cannot deliver to a P.O. Box.)

School/Institution
Name & Title
Street
County
City State Zip
Authorized Signature and Title

☐ Check Enclosed   ☐ Visa   ☐ MasterCard
Card Number   Expiration Date   Signature

Bill to: (Please type or print clearly.)

School/Institution
Name & Title
Street
County
City State Zip
Phone

Grade Level	Resource Manuals	Price	Qty	Total Price	Check-Ups™ (Set of 30) Booklets	Price	Qty	Total Price	Overhead Transparencies	Price	Qty	Total Price	Classpacks	Price	Qty	Total Price
					Daily Math Reinforcers™											
K	D9-80110	$21.95			D9-80120	$91.95			D9-80130	$64.95				NA		
1	D9-80111	$21.95			D9-80121	$91.95			D9-80131	$64.95			D9-80141	$113.90		
2	D9-80112	$21.95			D9-80122	$91.95			D9-80132	$64.95			D9-80142	$113.90		
3	D9-80113	$21.95			D9-80123	$91.95			D9-80133	$64.95			D9-80143	$113.90		
4	D9-80114	$21.95			D9-80124	$91.95			D9-80134	$64.95			D9-80144	$113.90		
5	D9-80115	$21.95			D9-80125	$91.95			D9-80135	$64.95			D9-80145	$113.90		
6	D9-80116	$21.95			D9-80126	$91.95			D9-80136	$64.95			D9-80146	$113.90		
7	D9-80117	$21.95			D9-80127	$91.95			D9-80137	$64.95			D9-80147	$113.90		
8	D9-80118	$21.95			D9-80128	$91.95			D9-80138	$64.95			D9-80148	$113.90		
					Daily Science Reinforcers™											
1	D9-80311	$21.95			D9-80321	$91.95			D9-80331	$64.95			D9-80341	$113.90		
2	D9-80312	$21.95			D9-80322	$91.95			D9-80332	$64.95			D9-80342	$113.90		
3	D9-80313	$21.95			D9-80323	$91.95			D9-80333	$64.95			D9-80343	$113.90		
4	D9-80314	$21.95			D9-80324	$91.95			D9-80334	$64.95			D9-80344	$113.90		
5	D9-80315	$21.95			D9-80325	$91.95			D9-80335	$64.95			D9-80345	$113.90		
6	D9-80316	$21.95			D9-80326	$91.95			D9-80336	$64.95			D9-80346	$113.90		
					Daily Reading Reinforcers™											
1	D9-80211	$23.95			D9-80221	$91.95			D9-80231	$64.95			D9-80241	$115.90		
2	D9-80212	$23.95			D9-80222	$91.95			D9-80232	$64.95			D9-80242	$115.90		
3	D9-80213	$23.95			D9-80223	$91.95			D9-80233	$64.95			D9-80243	$115.90		
4	D9-80214	$23.95			D9-80224	$91.95			D9-80234	$64.95			D9-80244	$115.90		
5	D9-80215	$23.95			D9-80225	$91.95			D9-80235	$64.95			D9-80245	$115.90		
6	D9-80216	$23.95			D9-80226	$91.95			D9-80236	$64.95			D9-80246	$115.90		
					Daily Writing Reinforcers™											
1	D9-80411	$23.95			D9-80421	$91.95			D9-80431	$64.95			D9-80441	$115.90		
2	D9-80412	$23.95			D9-80422	$91.95			D9-80432	$64.95			D9-80442	$115.90		
3	D9-80413	$23.95			D9-80423	$91.95			D9-80433	$64.95			D9-80443	$115.90		
4	D9-80414	$23.95			D9-80424	$91.95			D9-80434	$64.95			D9-80444	$115.90		
5	D9-80415	$23.95			D9-80425	$91.95			D9-80435	$64.95			D9-80445	$115.90		
6	D9-80416	$23.95			D9-80426	$91.95			D9-80436	$64.95			D9-80446	$115.90		

Classpack:
- 1 Resource Manual
- 30 Check-Ups™ Booklets
- Free Wallchart

*SALES TAX: All orders should include state sales tax unless a tax exemption number or resale tax number is provided. Sales taxes are required in the states of CA, CT, DC, GA, IL, IN, IA, KS, LA, MD, MI, MN, MO, NC, NJ, NY, PA, SC, and VA. State laws in TX, WA, and WI mandate that sales tax be calculated on both merchandise and freight.

†SHIPPING CHARGES: All orders from individuals must be accompanied by payment or credit card information and should include 10% for shipping and handling charges within the continental U.S.; 20% for shipping charges outside the continental U.S. Actual shipping charges will apply if they exceed 20%. Please add $5.00 for shipping and handling on orders under $25.00.

Column 1 Sub-Total _____
Column 2 Sub-Total _____
Column 3 Sub-Total _____
Column 4 Sub-Total _____

Columns 1, 2, 3, 4 Total _____
*Sales Tax _____
†Shipping _____
TOTAL _____

This order form may be reproduced.